Take an adventure through history with three FREE historical novels from James Rada, Jr.

WRITE NOW!

How to Make a Living Freelance Writing

by
James Rada, Jr.

Other books by James Rada, Jr.

Non-Fiction

- Battlefield Angels: The Daughters of Charity Work as Civil War Nurses
- Beyond the Battlefield: Stories from Gettysburg's Rich History
- Clay Soldiers: One Marine's Story of War, Art, & Atomic Energy
- Echoes of War Drums: The Civil War in Mountain Maryland
- The Last to Fall: The 1922 March, Battles & Deaths of U.S. Marines at Gettysburg
- Looking Back: True Stories of Mountain Maryland
- Looking Back II: More True Stories of Mountain Maryland
- No North, No South: The Grand Reunion at the 50th Anniversary of the Battle of Gettysburg
- Saving Shallmar: Christmas Spirit in a Coal Town
- Secrets of Catoctin Mountain: Little-Known Stories & Hidden History Along Catoctin Mountain
- Secrets of Garrett County: Little-Known Stories & Hidden History of Maryland's Westernmost County
- Secrets of the C&O Canal: Little-Known Stories & Hidden History Along the Potomac River
- Secrets of the Gettysburg Battlefield: Little-Known Stories & Hidden History from the Gettysburg Battlefield
- Secrets of Washington County: Little-Known Stories & Hidden History Where Western Maryland Starts

Fiction

- Between Rail and River
- Canawlers
- Frostburg Burning
- Lock Ready
- October Mourning
- Smoldering Betrayal
- Strike the Fuse
- The Rain Man

WRITE NOW!

How to Make a Living Freelance Writing

by
James Rada, Jr.

AIM

PUBLISHING

A division of AIM Publishing Group

HOW TO MAKE A LIVING FREELANCE WRITING

Published by AIM Publishing, a division of AIM Publishing Group.
Gettysburg, Pennsylvania.
Printed in the United States of America.
First printing: December 2022.

ISBN 978-1-7352890-6-9

AIM

PUBLISHING

315 Oak Lane • Gettysburg, Pennsylvania 17325

CONTENTS

1

INTRODUCTION

Things don't look so great for writers nowadays. Although the U.S. Bureau of Labor Statistics estimates that the number of reporter jobs will increase by six percent over the next decade, the market doesn't seem to be showing it. A Pew research study showed that newsrooms in the country had lost 26 percent of their employees between 2008 and 2020.

So if you want to find work as a writer, you need to create your own opportunities and not depend on someone else to give you a job. Work is still available for freelance writers if you know how to look for it and go after it when you do find it.

You can even make a better living as a freelance writer than as a newspaper reporter, though it's not an easy career choice. One report I read said that 84 percent of freelance writers can't earn a living solely as a freelance writer. The potential is there, but you need to make it a goal to be part of the 16 percent.

However, TheTilt.com looked at content creators across a variety of industries in its publication *The*

Creator Next Door. "Few creators are striking it rich, but many are earning enough to support themselves. Just over half (51%) of full-time content creators say they're making enough to at least support themselves. Of that group, 19% support more than one person," Joe Pulizzi, founder of The Tilt, said.

Newsroom employment in the United States declined 26% between 2008 and 2020

Number of U.S. newsroom employees in news industries, in thousands

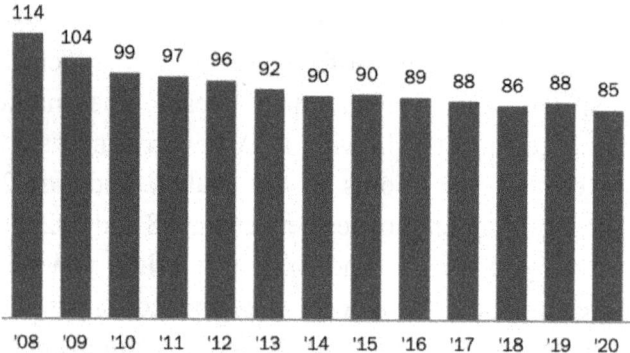

Note: The OEWS survey is designed to produce estimates by combining data collected over a three-year period. Newsroom employees include news analysts, reporters and journalists; editors; photographers; and television, video and film camera operators and editors. News industries include newspaper publishers; radio broadcasting; television broadcasting; cable and other subscription programming; and other information services, the best match for digital-native news publishers.
Source: Pew Research Center analysis of Bureau of Labor Statistics Occupational Employment and Wage Statistics data.

Reprinted with permission. "U.S. newsroom employment has fallen 26% since 2008." Pew Research Center, Washington, D.C. (July 13, 2021) https://www.-pewresearch.org/fact-tank/2021/07/13/u-s-newsroom-employment-has-fallen-26-since-2008/.

I've been a professional writer since 1988, although all that time hasn't been as a freelance writer. I've written novels, short stories, magazine articles, technical materials, and newspaper columns. I've also created ads, brochures, television commercials, and radio spots; edited magazines; and probably done some more stuff I'm forgetting.

It's all part of being a freelance writer. You are your own boss, doing work for several different clients. You choose your own clients and assignments, but you usually have to keep a lot of projects moving at once in order to earn a living. If you wait until one project is finished before beginning your next one, you won't be able to make enough money to live on unless that one project requires you to work full time.

Over the years, I've had two freelancing careers that focused on different aspects of the business. The first time I worked as a full-time freelance writer, which lasted seven years. I did it because I was tired of working for a company—or at least a boss—who treated employees poorly. I decided to set out on my own. During this stint as a freelance writer, I primarily did technical editing, advertising copywriting, and articles for trade magazines.

I managed to make a living at it, but if there's an easy way and a hard way of doing something, my first freelancing career was definitely the hard way. I had almost no clue as to what I was doing, and so I limped along, just managing to get by and certainly not having any fun doing the work.

Then my wife and I decided to start our family, and she wanted to cut back on her work hours at her job. My income at the time fluctuated too widely, and with the additional expenses that we would soon have, I realized that I needed to go back to work for a weekly check. I found a job as a newspaper reporter. It certainly didn't pay well, although I enjoyed the work.

My current freelance writing career came not from choice but necessity. After working for eight years as a newspaper reporter and editor, the newspaper I was working for shut down, and my family was not in a position to move so that I could write full time for another newspaper.

Luckily, I had already been doing some part-time freelance writing for a few months prior to the newspaper's closure, and I was able to hit the ground running. Plus, technology had improved between my two freelance writing careers. I found it much easier and less costly to work remotely with clients across the country. For instance, I saved a lot of money on postage because e-mail was now the predominant way to communicate with editors and clients. Online databases cut down on my need to travel to various places to research a topic.

I now make a good living as a full-time freelance writer, and I am loving my work. I am not alone in that feeling. The Tilt found that just one percent of the creators they surveyed regretted their decision.

So, you may work hard and struggle to get traction in the writing and publishing world, but you won't mind it because you'll love the work. As Pulizzi noted in *The Creator Next Door,* "Content creators may be the most satisfied workers on the planet."

This book is adapted from a class I've been teaching at a couple of community colleges and a local arts council for the past ten years. As such, I've incorporated the changes I've made to it over the years based on feedback from my students. I've also written it to answer a lot of the questions that my students commonly ask. Hopefully, I've answered questions you might have. If not, feel free to e-mail me at *jimrada@yahoo.com.*

Throughout the book you will see short breakouts titled Strategy Tips. These are suggestions for a way you might start using the concepts taught in the book. It's not the only way to do things, but it's a way that I've found works, and it's worth a try to see if it works for you.

At a time when the country was in a recession, I have seen my business grow by more than 15 percent each year, and I expect it to do so again this year.

Whether you are looking for full-time income like I needed or would just like to make a few hundred extra bucks a month, this book can show you how to lay out your freelance writing career path.

WHY FREELANCE?

When I mention freelance writing, what type of writing jumps to mind? Blogs? Newspaper columns? Magazine features? Writing about cats, gardening, food? That is probably the type of freelancing that you should focus to start your work as a freelancer. Meanwhile, you'll want to keep your eyes open for other opportunities where you can put your writing skills to work to increase your experience and grow your freelance-writing business.

Freelance writing is simply someone paying you to write something, whether it's an ad, novel, or article. They are paying for the writing, not you. Here are some of the types of freelance writing I've done:

- Newsletters
- Newspaper columns
- Radio scripts
- Newspaper articles
- Catalogs
- Magazine articles
- Press releases

- Short stories
- Novels
- Magazine editing
- Ads
- Teaching
- Brochures
- Blogs
- Direct mail packages
- Public speaking

Do any of these things appeal to you? You may be able to come up with some other types of writing not on my list, and that's great. Perhaps, it is an under-served market you can fill. The list of things I've written certainly isn't all-encompassing. For instance, I don't do poetry or movie scripts. That's not to say I never will, but it isn't something I want to do at this point. Lots of things need to be written, and you can be the person doing that writing. You just need to find them.

Freelance writing has plenty of advantages that make it the perfect job for me, and hopefully, you. That doesn't mean there aren't drawbacks that you need to consider. First and foremost, it is hard work that requires you to wear several different hats. You can't sit around waiting for inspiration to strike. Nor can you only write while someone else handles your marketing, sales, production, bookkeeping, etc.

Let's look at the advantages to being a freelance

writer. Some are specific to freelancing and some are the advantages of working for yourself. You may even come up with some that I've missed. These are the ones that I've found that I like as a full-time freelance writer.

Advantages

You can set your own hours. – I am a morning person. I am up early ready to work. When my kids were younger, I used to get a couple hours of work done before I took a break to get them ready for school. Once they were out the door, I would work some more, then take a break to exercise, do something fun, do a house errand, or something else. As a freelance writer, you are your own boss. You know the work that needs to be done, and you should set your time accordingly. Your clients don't care when you are working, only that you are completing their projects on time. If you are freelancing part-time, you can still set your own hours, but you will need to fit them around your full-time work schedule.

You can work from home. – Having a home office has tax advantages, but you will also appreciate it when the weather is bad. On snowy winter mornings, I don't have to worry about digging my car out from the snow and creeping to work on snow-covered streets. I simply walk down the hallway to my home office. The only traffic I have to worry about is tripping over one of the family cats. However, it can be hard to concentrate in the evenings or mornings when there are other people moving around and making noise. If that's the case with you, you might need to set rules and ask your family to honor them. It can be something as simple as opening or closing your door: if your office door is open, they can come in; if it is closed, they need to stay out. Also, unlike working in a newsroom or office, I can play music I like or listen to old-time radio shows. If that is distracting to you, you can work in silence. It's your choice.

You choose your work. – As a freelance writer, you choose your work in two ways. 1) You'll send out queries, pitching story ideas to publications or companies about your abilities. You only send out ideas to publications and companies you're interested in writing for. 2) Once editors start contacting you about writing for them, you can choose which ones you want to write for and which ones you want to pass on.

Strategy Tip: *While you can turn down freelance writing assignments, if you pass on too many, the client might lose interest in working with you. Make yourself as available as you can to fill a client's writing needs because if you don't, someone else will.*

You determine your income – When I was working for other people, I had employers tell me, "I wish I could give you a bigger raise, but the company's not allowing it." My wife had a job once where all the raises in her department had to average out to a departmental percentage, which meant for one person to get a larger-than-average raise, one of her co-workers had to get a smaller-than-average raise. As a freelance writer, your income depends on you and you alone. If you're a hard worker and inventive about finding revenue streams or very productive, this is an encouraging prospect. My income has grown by double-digit percentages each year I've freelanced this second time. As a part-time freelance writer, you'll find those freelancing checks nice gifts in the mail that can easily add up to a couple thousand dollars to your income annually.

You enjoy tax advantages – You get some nice tax advantages as a freelance writer. If you do your writing from a home office, you can write off part of your mortgage and home expenses on your taxes. You can pad your retirement by setting up your own company retirement plan. I have also found that there are a lot of things I use in my business that I might otherwise have bought: computer, software, new desk chair, printer ink, etc. They all become tax deductions when used in my business.

You are not dependent on one revenue stream – When you work for a company and get one paycheck a week, you are dependent on that company. Your fortunes rise or fall with the company's success. I found that out the hard way when the newspaper I was working for as an editor had to shut down. I was lucky in that instance because I had some freelance income already established. I used my time while unemployed to build that freelance income up to a full-time job. As a freelance writer, you can work in a variety of fields and in a variety of media. Each assignment will earn you a paycheck, some large and others small, but when you are getting a half a dozen checks a week, they will add up to a decent income.

Disadvantages

While freelance writing is a great job and one that I love, it is not perfect. Here are some drawbacks I have found working as a freelance writer:

Your cash flow can be inconsistent – When you work for someone, you get paid regularly: once a week, every two weeks, etc. You can budget for how you will meet any of your household expenses. As a freelance writer, it can be hard to know when your next check is coming in the mail. I have clients who will pay a portion up front and the remainder on completion of the project. Other clients pay 30 or 60 days after publication of an article, and the publication of an article might be up to a year after I have submitted it. Trying to balance my cash flow so that

I've got enough money each month is impossible if rely on cash in hand. I've developed a budget for expenses. I put all of my income into a savings account, and then at the beginning of the following month, I transfer the budget amount into my checking account and pay my bills. It's the only way I can work it. Think of it as giving yourself a paycheck.

Freelancing is lonely work – Although you will go to meetings and do interviews for articles, for the most part, freelance writing is lonely work. You sit alone in a room in front of a computer. That's why I like to have old-time radio shows playing while I work. It provides background voices so I don't feel quite so lonely. It's also why I like to get out and interact when I can. I attend a weekly writers group to enjoy the company of other writers.

You need to be disciplined – Working at home, it's easy to get distracted. There are TV shows on that you want to watch or dishes piling up in the sink that need washing. Even housework can seem more appealing than the hard work of putting together an article or a marketing campaign. There's also the problem of friends who think you're always free. They call or stop in when you're working. You have to be able to set limits and goals for your work day and stick to them.

You can easily overwork – It's easy to work too long and wind up burned out. When I was starting out, I worked long hours to grow my business. Now, when I've got free time, I find myself at a loss for something to do. It's hard to turn off the work sometimes, but you've got to, or you can burn out. Develop some hobbies, in particular, active ones that will provide you with the physical activity you need.

You need to learn to withstand rejection – As a full-time freelance writer, you are going to be sending out query letters and manuscripts multiple times during the week. You'll be calling on clients looking for work. You need to have a strong ego to withstand rejection (and you will get rejected). Not even the best writers have a perfect track record of placing all their stories.

Strategy Tip: *I fight the feeling of rejection by not focusing on it. I look forward to the next acceptance. If I have an editor turn down a story, I don't worry over why the editor rejected it. It may not have been a good fit for the publication. I may have caught the editor on a bad day. The publication's budget might not allow it. I don't worry. I turn right around and submit the idea to another publication.*

You are responsible for everything – As a freelance writer, you are generally going to be a one-person show. You won't be able to simply write articles and stories. You will need to market yourself, keep the books, pay bills, answer phones, etc. The Tilt.com survey, *The Creator Next Door,* found that "On average, full-time content creators spend about half their time creating content. The other half is spent on business issues like content distribution, promotion, marketing, sales, and administration/operations." It is all part of the nuts and bolts of running your own company, which is what your freelancing career is… a business. If you do reach a point where you are earning enough, you can farm some of those jobs out, such as hiring a bookkeeper or virtual assistant. Those services cost, though, so it is usually best that you do them yourself while you are building your business.

Why Employers Like Freelancers

Part of being successful as a freelancer is understanding what role you play with an employer and how you help them. Knowing that, you can fulfill the role better, improve customer satisfaction, retain clients, and get more work.

Magazines use freelance writers because they provide new sources of ideas and different perspectives. Take a magazine like *Pennsylvania Magazine*, for which I have written many articles. The magazine seeks to cover the events and history of the entire Commonwealth of Pennsylvania. If the magazine had to hire staff to do all of that, it would be expensive. Not only would the magazine have to pay the full-time salaries and benefits of all the staff that would be needed, it would also have to pay for the cost to travel to locations across the state or to run regional offices. Instead, the magazine has people sending the editor ideas from which he or she can pick and choose.

Also, the magazine doesn't have to pay employment costs for freelance writers. The general estimate is that the cost of benefits and employer taxes paid by an employer on behalf of an employee account for an additional 30–40 percent above the employee's salary. For example, a newspaper reporter earning $30,000 a year in salary, probably costs the newspaper $39,000 to $42,000 a year to employ when the value of benefits is included. That reporter works five days a week for 50 weeks a year writing an average of one story a day. That's 250 stories a year. That means those stories cost the newspaper an average of $162 each. However, that same newspaper probably pays freelance columnists and writers only $75 to $100 a story.

Companies that use freelance marketing writers and copywriters do so for much the same reason. It costs them less than using an advertising agency. An agency works their operating costs into the amounts they charge their clients, and maintaining an office with four or five employees creates a lot more overhead than a single freelance writer working in his or her dcn at home. The company also gets more direct service from a freelance writer, and the company can also get a higher level of subject expertise depending on the writer they select.

So, freelancers save their clients money while giving them greater expertise. That creates a strong bargaining position for freelancers.

FIRST STEPS

Some writers jump into freelance writing full time. Some writers are forced into it. If you have the option, ease into it. Your blood pressure will thank you.

Start by working at freelance writing as a side gig. Build up a reputation and get some clients who like to use you regularly. They will form the foundation upon which you can build your business. Get examples clippings of your published work (called clippings in the industry) to use them to help you get future work.

These things can take some time, so doing them while you are drawing a paycheck from a full-time job will reduce your stress when you do make the jump to full-time freelancing. It will also get you used to running a freelance writing business. You can work out the kinks that come with running your own business before you commit to it.

When you do go full time as a freelance writer, things will be stressful enough. Doing what I'm suggesting will minimize your problems.

Making the move to working as your own boss is going to be scary no matter how you do it, though. You have to take on a new mindset. You are no longer an employee who is working within a particular department of a company while others do their work in other departments. You are going to be doing everything. If you don't work, you don't get paid.

Many writers fear not being able to get enough ideas day after day, dealing with the pressure of too many deadlines, or enduring an editor who ravages your work. I've faced all those feelings and more at one time or another. Some of them, I've faced more than once. I can tell you this. Keep yourself focused on the end goal of building a career. Keep working toward that, and those fears will eventually pass away. They are just blips on your career path when you are focused on the long-term goal.

Planning for a Business

Even if you pursue freelance writing as a part-time job, you have to consider it a business because it is. You may think that you will only have to worry about writing articles, books, ads, etc., but there are other business functions that will need to happen to know what works and stay on the right side of the Internal Revenue Service.

Many experts will say you need a business plan, and I believe you need one… of a sort.

A formal business plan will be necessary if you want to get bank funding or an investor, but freelance writers rarely require this. Besides, your goal is to keep your overhead low to maximize your profit. You don't want to have to worry about making a loan payment as you are working hard to earn enough to cover your other expenses.

My business has grown as my earnings have increased. I eased into the work and did not jump into it in a sink-or-swim situation. This put a lot less stress on me as I developed my client base. Additionally, most of the up-front costs you might need as a freelance writer can easily be covered with a few credit card purchases, although I would recommend saving up for those things for the same reason I said to avoid a loan payment.

However, there are times when you might need to use your credit card. When I started indie publishing books and needed a few thousand dollars for my first book printing, I charged it and then made paying off the charge a priority for the next few months. It was the simple way to go. I didn't have to fill out paperwork and wait for a loan approval. I just pulled out my Visa card.

If you do go this route, you will need to be disciplined enough to make sure you use the proceeds from your business to pay off the charges.

Having said that, I do have a business plan, but it is an informal one. A bank would never accept it, but it works for me. Each year, I write a list of my goals for the year. Which books will I publish and when will they be released? What do I project my earnings to be? How will that amount be split between my revenue streams? How many articles do I want to have published? How many will be in new markets? They should be measurable goals as much as possible. I set reasonable goals that will make me work to achieve them, but aren't out of the realm of possibility. Under each goal, I write how I plan to achieve it.

My annual plan is a living document that I will revisit throughout the year and adjust as needed. My goal is not to use it to obtain credit, but to keep me focused on improving my business.

Free Work?

If you are new to professional writing, you may need to write your first freelance assignments for free or at a very low price in order to get clippings (another good reason to start freelancing on a part-time basis). You can then use these clippings to show higher paying clients the type of work you are capable of writing. You might also need to do this even if you are experienced but are trying to break into new areas where you don't have any experience.

When I was starting out as a freelancer my first time, I had biotechnology experience, but I wanted to expand into other areas. I did this by writing a movie review column for a local newspaper and a financial tips column for a senior newspaper. I did these for free for about a year. I also ghost wrote a sports medicine column for a client. They paid me to write the column, and a local sports newspaper printed it. Although the newspaper didn't pay, I made my money from the client, and I got experience writing about a new topic.

Capitalization

Starting out freelancing on a part-time basis allows you time to build up your savings account so that you will have money to live on while you are waiting for checks from published articles to fill your mailbox. This initial savings is called capitalization, and under-capitalization is the main reason that businesses fail within five years of starting up. While freelance writing doesn't require a great amount of capitalization, it does require some.

Figure out your needs for about three to six months. How much money will you need to live on and cover your writing expenses during that time? This is how much you want to save before you make the jump to full time. It will be a sizable chunk of money, but it might be a few months before payments for projects you do in the first months of your business start coming in.

I compare this type of easing into the full-time

writing life as being the frog in the pot as the water is slowly heating up. However, in the end, you won't be cooked, you will be a full-time freelancer and comfortable in the position.

The first time I freelanced full time, I jumped into it with little preparation, and I had to scramble like crazy to make ends meet. I had thought I was prepared, but there's a lot more to being your own boss than you might expect. You have to get used to making your own decisions about your business, establishing contacts, setting up your financial books, etc. By easing into the work, you will run into these things over an extended period of time and learn how to deal with them.

The second time I started freelancing full time, I had already started writing as a side gig. I had a lot of the elements in place, so when the newspaper I was writing for closed, I was able to make the transition with only a slight bump.

Building a Workspace

Some writers will say they can write anywhere. While that is true, there are advantages to having a dedicated workspace.

Your workspace is where you keep everything related to your business, and it can be located anywhere. When I lived in a small apartment, my office was a tiny cubby area in the kitchen that I believe was supposed to be a pantry. It was barely large enough for my desk and chair, and even then, when I sat in the chair I stuck out into the kitchen.

Nowadays, my office is a room. I was tempted to show you a picture, but I didn't want you dropping this book in shock at how cluttered it can look. I have my desk, printer, computer, and filing cabinet as the main pieces in the room. However, I also have lots of bookshelves filled with my research books and my own inventory. Often the floor is cluttered with boxes of inventory that I take to shows where I sell books.

Optimally, your workspace should be a place that offers you privacy and the ability to close yourself off from the rest of the household. The advantage of a door is that it can separate you from the house so you can concentrate and let others in the house know you are working. It also offers you the opportunity to close off your work life at the end of the day.

Having a dedicated home office offers financial advantages. You aren't having to pay for office space, and you can take a home office deduction on your taxes. Consult a tax professional as to whether this is applicable and beneficial in your case. You will probably appreciate this more in the early years of your business when you are working hard to make a profit with a small customer base.

Your space needs to have a phone, computer, and Internet access. One suggestion I have heard is to have two computers: one you do most of your work on that is not connected to Internet (to avoid distractions) and one that is connected, so you can use it for research.

Strategy Tip: *In an effort to minimize your start-up costs, consider buying furniture and even your computer used. You can probably find a usable desk, chair, lamp, filing cabinet, or whatever you might want at a yard sale. As your business grows, you can upgrade your purchases and make the area a more comfortable place to work.*

Finally, talk to the insurance company that holds your homeowner's or renter's policy for what you might need. Most likely, you will need to get a business rider on your homeowner's policy so that any business equipment losses you might have from theft, fire, flood, etc. are covered by insurance.

WHAT TYPE OF FREELANCER ARE YOU?

By this point, you may wonder whether you are suited for the freelancing life. I found this evaluation in *Publish Your Own Novel* by Connie Shelton. (Sadly, this book is now out of print, but you can check out her books at ConnieShelton.com) Her version is for writers considering indie publishing in the 1990s, but I adapted it a bit with permission to apply to freelancers today. Choose whichever answer best fits you and your personality and write the number.

Independence:
1. I want to be my own boss. I am highly moti-

vated and a self-starter.

2. I'm fairly independent, but I don't want to make all the decisions by myself.

3. I am not a self-starter. I would rather have someone else worry about the problems.

Entrepreneurial Spirit:

1. I like controlling the direction of my projects.

2. I want to give input, but would like someone else to help with the decisions.

3. I do not want too much responsibility. I'd rather someone else handled it all.

Financial Status:

1. I have money I can afford to risk in a business of my own.

2. I have great ideas but not much money. I could do it with some outside investors.

3. I want to be assured of payment for my writing.

Business Knowledge:

1. I have some experience in business or management.

2. I have a general understanding of business, but I could use some help.

3. I have no business experience and can't even balance my checkbook.

Self-Promotion:
1. I want the world to know about what I can do for their business or magazine.
2. Although I'm normally shy, I know that I need to promote myself to get business, so I will do it.
3. I have a hard time promoting my own work.

Public Appearances:
1. I am comfortable speaking in front of audiences when I feel I have something important to say.
2. I need more confidence with public appearances but am willing to learn.
3. Even the idea of attending a meeting makes me queasy.

Selling Skills:
1. I enjoy the satisfaction of selling a product I believe in.
2. I don't like direct sales but can promote a product through mail order, advertising or via wholesalers.
3. Writing is an art. I don't feel that it is proper to openly solicit sales.

Tally up the how many 1s, 2s, and 3s you picked. If you checked mostly 1s, you're an ideal candidate for freelancing full time. It is probably where you'd be happiest. If you checked mostly 2s with some 1s, you can still be successful at freelancing, but you might want to get a little outside help. If you checked mostly 3s, you're probably going to be more comfortable with a traditional writing job and doing a little freelancing on the side. This doesn't mean you can't learn new stuff. However, if you chose 3 for the last 2 questions, you might want to reconsider writing for publication.

Just to let you know, when I originally took this test, my score was about evenly split between 1s and 2s. I was willing to learn, though, and worked hard to get better. Now, when I take the test, I score nearly all 1s.

Don't give up. Get better.

Specialist vs. Generalist

You can specialize in certain areas of writing (i.e., technical writing, celebrity interviews, copywriting) or you can be a generalist who writes a bit of everything.

The first time I started working as a freelance writer, I specialized. I had a few clients lined up to write for when I made the jump from employee to freelance writer. They were all biotechnology companies. The work paid well (specialized writing generally pays better than general writing), but it put me in a specialized area of doing biotechnology writing and some science writing because all my experience was in that field. I've always felt like it was putting all my eggs in one basket. If I had still been doing just that type of writing when the biotechnology market began to shrink and companies consolidated, I could have found myself struggling for work. I was already working for a newspaper when that happened, though.

The second time I launched my freelance writing career, I did it as a generalist. I write in a lot of different areas and rarely turn down an assignment, especially if it allows me to write on a new subject or in a new market.

However, over the years, I have found that there are certain areas that I like to write about more than others. While I am still a generalist, I do have areas in which I have more experience. For example, I sent a query for a story about the Spanish Flu to a regional magazine. The editor liked the idea, but wanted it to look more at preventing the modern flu. So, I wrote the story from that angle and turned it into a health story. This lead to me writing another health article for the same magazine about fighting the common cold. Now, I have two clippings and experience writing about health and medical subjects that I can show to an editor if I want to write another health story.

As a side note, the above example is a good reason why you should query an article before you write it. An editor may like the idea, but may want a slightly different angle to the story. If you've already written the article, you will have to rewrite it.

This is the first page of an article that started out as a story about Spanish Flu, but it morphed into an article about fighting the flu. It led to a second health article for the same magazine. Image courtesy of Hagerstown Magazine.

Your first goal starting out should be to build your business. Take any assignment that offers to pay you for your writing. You might find yourself liking a new area of writing or you might hate the work. At this early stage in your career, you can't afford to be too choosy. So try it all if the opportunity arises.

Look for assignments that you not only like but also ones that you can do fast and efficiently. This will help you increase your income without having to increase drastically the amount of time that you work.

Once you have found more than enough work to keep you busy during your work week, then you can begin prioritizing the assignments you want to take and dropping the work that isn't a good fit with your personality or doesn't pay as much as other assignments.

Strategy Tip: *If an assignment comes along that will give you experience with a new topic or give you a great clipping when published, consider taking the assignment even if you have to do it for free. The experience and clipping can help make up for the lack of payment down the road.*

Know Your Audience

Freelance writing can be divided into three general areas, based on who will be reading the piece.

Commercial – This is public writing. It includes stories, novels, magazines, etc. This type of writing does not generally pay as well as other types of writing, but you get more recognition from it. It is also easier to get your foot in the door doing this type of writing.

Business – Business writing is ads, brochures, direct mail, and sales letters, among others. You need more refined skills to understand what the different forms of writing entail and an understanding of marketing to be an effective business writer, which is why it pays better than public writing. The readers of business writing are people interested in a business, product, or service.

Scientific – Scientific writing, as the name implies, can be very technical. You need to break things down and rebuild them. It's a very precise type of writing and requires a good foundation in the scientific or technical field about which you are writing. It often involves writing manuals and spec sheets. It pays well.

People tend to specialize in one of these areas. During my first stint as a freelance writer, I specialized in scientific writing involving biotechnology and its related fields. Writing for those types of companies made up about 80 percent of my work. During this current work as a freelance writer, my work is more public writing with a little business writing.

Let's look at the types of writing and how you can get started with each of them.

COMMERCIAL WRITING

Commercial writing is what most people think of when they think about freelance writing. It is articles in newspapers and magazines that appeal to a general audience.

Where to Find Ideas

Before you write an article, you have to have an idea. Hopefully, at some point in your career, you will have editors approaching you to write their ideas. It's a sure sale and saves you some time coming up with the idea, but it might not be an idea that excites you.

That's why you want to have your own list of ideas. Once you train yourself, you will find ideas in just about everything because they are all around you. Things you see, do, hear. Your personal history and life experiences. These can also become the basis for article ideas.

When I was a newspaper reporter, I noticed other

reporters fell into one of two categories: either they stuck to their beat, covered meetings, and created as many stories from a meeting as they could, or they went out into the area they were covering, talked to people, and looked around to see what was happening. The latter tended to write stories of greater interest.

Pay attention to the world around you. Network with others, both professionally and socially. Think about what you read. You will start to get ideas.

A member of my writing group is a wonderful magazine writer, and she is great at finding ideas all around her. We recently had a new member attend one of our meetings. When this woman started telling the group about herself and her day job, the magazine writer started questioning her to get more details. Our group leader laughed and said, "I know that tone. She thinks she's got a new story idea."

Something as simple as a person's job, which that person probably thought was mundane, triggered something in the magazine writer, and she thought she had a new story idea. Maybe something will come of it. Maybe not.

It might not be that person's job that becomes the focus of the eventual story she writes. It could be that there is a different angle to the story that can be written about. Those different angles can give the idea a fresh look.

When I was a reporter, I used to attend town meetings. I got to know familiar faces at these meetings, including a Catholic sister. Once, when we were talking, I mentioned I liked history, and she started telling about the work the Daughters of Charity did as Civil War nurses. This caught my attention, and when I looked into it, I found that although the Daughters of Charity made up the bulk of the Catholic sisters who served during the Civil War, their stories were often overlooked because they were called Sisters of Charity or Sisters of Mercy, which were different orders. I decided to write specifically about the Daughters of Charity, and it became the basis for my nonfiction book, *Battlefield Angels*.

Strategy Tip: *Think about holidays and anniversaries of events. These can make a good story for a magazine, but you will need to pitch a timely idea at least three months before the holiday or anniversary (six months is preferred).*

Swipe Files

Once you start getting more ideas than you can write, create a swipe file.

When I read an interesting article or learn a fact that catches my attention, I file it away in my swipe file. Yes, this can be a literal file. I have both a physical and a digital swipe file.

I don't particularly like the name because it implies you're stealing the idea. You aren't.

When you want to prepare a meal, you remove the ingredients you need from your refrigerator or pantry, combine them in a certain way to come up with your meal. By adding or removing ingredients, you can create a different meal. That's the way a swipe file works. The articles and facts are your ingredients. You combine them in different ways to create different stories. Maybe I should call it an idea pantry instead of a swipe file.

Strategy Tip: *Carry a small memo notebook and pen with you in your pocket or purse. If you find yourself asking a question about something or wondering about something, write it down. If you find yourself impressed or disappointed with something, write it down. Many of these things can be story ideas that you can turn into articles.*

What is interesting is that I could give you my swipe file, and you would probably come up with different stories to write than I would. That's the chef's talent for creating a delicious dish or, in our case, the writer's eye.

I have large files of ideas for both books and articles. Sadly, I don't often go to the files for inspiration because I can see ideas all around me. It's a shame, really, because I know there are some gems in those files.

Now that you have an idea for an article, let's look at where you can sell it. With commercial writing, there are three primary areas: the Internet, magazines, and newspapers.

The Internet

The easiest way I can think of to get started with freelance writing is to start with the Internet. There's lots of opportunity to write for websites, whether it's blog posts or full articles, and many sites don't require that you have a lot of experience. This low barrier to entry also means that these articles require less research and interviews. This makes it a good place for new writers. As you gain more experience, you can generally command higher pay.

A lot of new freelancers write for content mills such as eHow, Answerbag, and Livestrong. I've heard them dumped on a lot, but in general my experience with them has been decent, especially for beginning writers. I was registered with two content mills, although I haven't written for them for at least a decade because I can earn more money through other venues.

I have found that content mills offer plenty of work and pay regularly, which was the main reason I wrote for them when I was starting out as a full-time freelance writer. I wanted to make sure I had steady income while I was growing more profitable areas of my freelance career.

You might even start to get some good writing clips, which you will be able to show to other editors as you seek better paying work. Most of the work I wouldn't use for clips, but I did get to write for USAToday.com and the San Francisco Chronicle website through a content mill. While I might not include the articles I wrote for them among my clippings, I'm more than happy to name drop them in my query letters.

I didn't find the writing for content mills particularly interesting or challenging. Pay ranged from $3 to $80 per article or short post. When I was writing for the content mills, I tended to write business and financial articles that paid $17.50 for 400–500 words. That's less than 5 cents a word. Not great. However, because these articles were simple and used a format, I could average, with edits, about 1.5 articles an hour so then you're looking at more than $26 an hour.

Content mills have improved since I wrote for them. They offer a greater variety of topics and better pay. Some include both copywriting, article writing, and blog post assignment on the same site. Others allow you to sell pre-written articles on their sites to their clients.

The key to making content mills pay is to turn the articles around quickly. It may not be engaging work, but it will help you pay the bills.

Content mills will teach you to write tightly. It will also teach you more about search engine optimization (SEO) and proper style.

To get a starter list of content mills to consider, check out Appendix A: Content Mills on page 205. Visit the sites and look over their articles to see if the topics that catch your attention. Then take a look at how much they pay and what their registration process is.

Strategy Tip: *Content mills often have a list of topics they want articles written about. I used to select all the articles around a particular topic so that I could use the same research for all the articles. This saved me a lot of time. I was able write the articles quicker, which meant I was making more money per hour.*

Another type of website for writers is a job-bidding site, such as eLance.com. I looked into using these sites, but when I saw how little people were getting paid for a lot of work, I had to shake my head. The goal of these sites is for the customer to get work for the cheapest price. That works opposite of my goal, which is to give the client quality writing at a fair price. The price that some of those projects were going for was ridiculous, like $1 for a 500-word article.

I don't see how anyone could make enough money to make these projects worth their time.

A third type of website you can write for is a pay-per-click site. Some content mills offer this option. If you like to write about hot-topic issues, then this option could be a profitable for you. You write an article on a topic of your choice, post it, and get paid by how many people read it or click on links on the same page. If you've ever watched a YouTube video, you are on a pay-per-click site. The creators get paid by how many people watch their videos (and the ads that YouTube adds to the video). Creators seem to get paid about a half cent per view. It may not seem like much, but 100,000 views would earn the creator about $500.

I wrote some articles for a content mill that offered pay-per-click rather a fixed rate as a payment option. I received royalty checks from these articles for years after they were published. In total, I made more money this way, but it was spread out over years.

Finally, there are sites that operate like a regular magazine. They offer you a fixed amount to write an article and purchase electronic rights or first-time publication rights. (We will talk more about rights later.) These sites often don't pay as much as a physical magazine does for articles, but they will pay more than a content mill.

Magazines

Consumer magazines are designed to appeal to large audiences. Trade magazines focus on occupations or industries. Between the two, you should be able to find one that is interested in any topic about which you might want to write.

When I graduated college, one of my first jobs was writing marketing materials for the National Solid Waste Management Association. They had several publications for members, but the two I remember are *Waste Age* and *Recycling Times.* They weren't magazines that you could find in Barnes & Noble, but those publications needed articles to fill each issue.

Just like you need to train yourself to look for the many ideas around you, you need to watch for potential markets for those ideas. Do you live near a bookstore or newsstand? Browse the magazines they carry and buy a copy of the ones you might want to write for. Look around the businesses you visit and notice where they might lay out magazines for customers. Do they have trade magazines on their desks? When you are browsing the web, do ads for magazines pop up that look interesting? They are all potential markets for you to investigate and query with your ideas.

Getting your articles into magazines requires that you write query letters, at least at first. I have some editors who contact me about writing stories for them, but it is only because they already know my work and suspect that I will be interested in the project. By and large, I am still submitting query letters.

Strategy Tip: *Create an online portfolio of your best writing clips. I created an online resume for myself that has download links for my list of clients, client comments, and PDF scans of magazine articles. When a potential client or editor asks to see samples of my work or my resume, I send them the link.*

Your best bet to break into magazine writing is with local and regional magazines. I love them and enjoy writing for them. Many states and major cities have a magazine focused on their area. These magazines don't have as wide a circulation as a national magazine, and they don't pay as well, but many of them are well designed. This means you can collect some good-looking writing clips.

The advantage for a freelance writer just starting out is that these magazines have a smaller circulation. This means they also have fewer writers submitting to them so a new writer has better odds of getting accepted.

If one magazine doesn't like your idea, you can tweak it to fit another magazine. This also increases your chances of having a magazine buy your article.

If a national magazine says "no" to your idea, you're going to be paid nothing. If a regional magazine says "no," you can send the idea to another regional magazine and another until you get an acceptance.

If there is a large magazine that you really want to have your article appear in, go ahead and plan an article they might like. However, just know that the larger a magazine is, the less likely it is to publish a new writer. It happens, but it is as rare as a high-school baseball player getting signed to a Major League Baseball team.

While these types of publications frequently use freelance writers, you need to know what type of material they are looking for. Department columns or feature articles? How-to articles? Lifestyle? Something else entirely? While you can get a feel for the types of articles a magazine runs by looking at it, you don't know whether freelance writers are used for that particular type of article.

Normally, for this information I would go to *Writer's Market,* which lists a lot of publications. It is not comprehensive, though. A lot of local and regional magazines fall through the cracks. Another technique I use is to search out magazines in a particular state and visit their websites.

I started writing magazine articles for a regional magazine called *Allegany Magazine.* From there, I worked up to statewide magazines and eventually national magazines. I still do most of my writing for regional magazines. It helps that a lot of the stories I want to write about have a strong regional angle, which makes them attractive to magazine editors in those regions.

Strategy Tip: *You can go for breadth or depth with magazine articles. I began with depth. I wrote multiple articles for a few magazines to develop strong relationships with those editors and learn how to write a good magazine article. Then I started going for breadth, writing for a wide variety of magazines. To date, I have had articles published in more than 140 magazines, newspapers, and newsletters.*

I believe regional magazines are holding their own in terms of circulation. This is personal observation because of the simple fact that they offer something other magazines can't: local stories. People interested in the Gettysburg lifestyle can find it best in *Celebrate Gettysburg* and not *Good Housekeeping*. How many national magazines carried stories about Johnny Depp and Amber Heard's defamation trial? How many carry stories about the upcoming elections? Judging by the covers I see at the grocery store, *Cosmopolitan* has written more articles about sex positions than there are positions. How many stories do health magazines run about getting flat abs?

Some of the many magazines where my articles have appeared. They are a mix of national, regional, and topical magazines.

Having sung the praises of regional magazines doesn't mean I'm against national magazines. I just look for ways to maximize my income with the least amount of effort. Getting articles accepted and published quickly, even if I'm paid only a portion of what a national magazine would pay, adds up. However, if you think your idea is a perfect match for a national magazine, query it. You might get lucky and get a big paycheck.

Strategy Tip: *Look for ideas that can be easily localized for multiple markets. If you sell the same idea to three or four regional markets, you can make the same as you would for one national publication. In addition, you can reuse much of the research and probably half of the article text. For instance, I wrote four articles about the Tuskegee Airmen, tailoring each article to the magazine's region by writing about the Tuskegee Airmen from that area.*

When I am considering writing an article, I consider three things: the pay, the market, and the story.

- **The pay** – I write for magazines because they pay better than newspapers and websites. I also enjoy how they look in print.
- **The market** – I will take less pay if the magazine is one that is new to me or one that I really want to get published in. For instance, I had an article published in the Maryland Historical Society Magazine and did not get paid for it. I did it because it's a prestigious, scholarly publication. I also knew it would be helpful when trying to market some of my books.
- **The story** – How badly do you want to see your story in print? It could mean you take an

assignment in a less prestigious or lower pay-ing magazine to see that happen.

Then it is a matter of deciding which factor means the most to you for a particular assignment. If you want to maximize the pay for an article, you will consider every market, and you will be willing to have an editor assign a particular story even if you don't like the topic. However, if where the piece is published is most important to you, you will be willing to take what that publication pays.

Query Letters

The ideal situation for you as a freelance writer is that editors will become so familiar with your work that they will start contacting you to write an article for their publication. I have a few editors who e-mail from time to time asking me to write a story for them. It is a wonderful feeling when that happens, and those are relationships I nurture.

Until that time arrives for you, you will need a query letter to get a writing assignment. Query letters are written to the editor of a magazine about the article you want to write.

There are two approaches that writers take in de-ciding where to send a query letter. 1) You can de-velop the idea first and then find a magazine where you think the story would fit. 2) You can find a magazine that you want to have your article published in, and plan an article that fits the magazine's editorial focus. The first approach is story driven. The second approach is market driven.

I have used both approaches to get work. I tend to use the former. I like coming up with my own ideas for articles. In doing so, I find I am more interested in the topic, which often means the story will turn out better.

This is much different from writing for newspapers where an editor will either assign you a story or you have a beat (a topic that a reporter is assigned to cover) that defines your story parameters. I used to come up with some great ideas when I was writing for newspapers, but I sometimes wasn't allowed to pursue the story because it wasn't part of my beat.

The drawback of magazine writing is that you have to write a query letter for each of those articles.

The sole purpose of a query letter is to hook editors, intrigue them, and make them want to learn more.

In that respect, a query and your article work the same way. They both need to hook the reader immediately. So that first paragraph in both is very important. Many times, I use the first paragraph of my query letter as the first paragraph of the article.

Once you have the paragraph written to intrigue the editor, make your proposal. What is the article you want to write? Does it have a title? Who will you be interviewing? What resources do you have? Talk about how your article will appeal to the magazine's audience.

In the next paragraph, list your qualifications to write the story. This can be a combination of previous experience with the topic, previous publications, awards, and honors. I will list previous publications similar to the one I am querying, and I will mention that I have won more than two dozen writing awards.

As a new freelance writer, you may not have previous credits or awards. So, what have you written? Any free articles? You don't need to say you didn't get paid, just who you wrote for. Have you done writing for the company where you are currently working? These could be listed as previous credits until you have more appropriate ones.

If all else fails, and you can't come up with any qualifications, then leave that paragraph out. But I am betting that you can come up with something.

Wrap it up. Your final paragraph needs to close things out with a request to write the article and an invitation for the editor to contact you. Don't forget to include your contact information!

If you are doing a letter by snail mail, make sure to include an SASE (self-addressed, stamped envelope), but it is faster and cheaper to use e-mail. Most editors also prefer this form of contact.

Check the writer or contributor guidelines, too. You may need to attach clippings of your previous work to your query. Only use published clips that look professional.

In considering your idea, check to see if the magazine has an editorial calendar. Some magazines have a theme for certain issues, and they plan far in advance for these issues. If you are trying to put together an article for a magazine, an editorial calendar can guide you on how to focus your article.

Strategy Tip: *One reason I worked to write for a large variety of publications was so that I could tailor my list of previous writing credits to the publication I was pitching. For example, if I'm pitching an idea to* Pennsylvania Magazine, *I might list* Johnstown, Pennsylvania History, *and* Celebrate Gettysburg *as previous publications I have written for. However, if I'm pitching a health story, I might mention* Hagerstown Magazine *(where I had two health stories published), my biotechnology work, and perhaps a magazine that published a story I wrote about the Spanish Flu. This helps show the editor that I'm familiar with the region or topic and that other editors have published my work in those areas.*

It is always best to send your query letter to a specific person. Look for the editor in charge of the department or type of article you are writing. If you can't find this person's name, you can send the query to the managing editor. If you can't find that name, send an e-mail to the general contact and ask for the name of the person who considers submissions.

For an example of an e-mail I used to get an assignment, look at Appendix B: Sample Query Letters on page 211.

Strategy Tip: *When e-mailing your query letter to an editor, consider the subject line as a way to hook the editor's attention. Editors see a lot of queries each week, so if you have an intriquing title or catchline about the story you can use, you stand a better chance of stopping an editor who is scanning the e-mail subject lines.*

Beginning on the next page, you will see an actual acceptance letter I received. It is just the way I received it except some personal information has been removed. Note the type of information you will be given when your idea is accepted. The story the editor expects, pay for the article, and deadline should be included in any acceptance letter. Other things in this letter, such as resources and format may not be a part of every acceptance letter you receive.

James Rada Jr.

ASSIGNMENT/AGREEMENT LETTER
FOR WRITER
Frederick Magazine

March 2, 2009

James Rada Jr.
[Address removed]

Re: Tranquility Farm feature – using horse thera-py to rehab war veterans

Dear Jim,

Thank you for agreeing to write the feature story for *Frederick Magazine's* April issue about the program at Tranquility Farm that uses horse riding to rehab veterans wounded in Iraq.

Story summary: Tranquility Farm sponsors programs that bring together rescued horses and people suffering from physical, mental or emotional injury. One of the newest programs at the farm is a unique project that aims to rehabilitate war veterans through horse therapy.

Source contact information:
Sarah Transeau, founder and president of Tranquility Farm

Payment: $500* [Paid upon publication (at the end of the published month.)]

*Payment includes any expenses for travel, telephone, fax or postage costs incurred by writer. Also, the fee paid to a writer for a magazine article includes *Frederick Magazine's* rights to use any portion of the assignment (or the entire article) on the magazine's Web site.

Deadline: By Monday, March 8. Please let me know immediately if you anticipate any problems meeting the deadline.

Resources
**Please list primary resources and telephone numbers, in case we need to contact anyone. Also, we suggest not relying on too many Web resources. Web resources you have used for information in the article should also be included with your list of primary resources.

How to Format Your Article for *Frederick Magazine*

[Remember, words inside brackets do not appear in the article.]
[Season/2008]
[Word Count: _____]

[Head] Please be sure to give your article a title.
[Subhead] Please be sure to give your article a subtitle, too.

[Writer's Byline] By Ayn Rand
[Photographer's Byline] Photography by Ansel Adams

As always, if you have any questions, please give me a call. (Before, you asked about style used in the magazine now. It is AP style.) Thanks for taking on this assignment; I look forward to reading it.

Sincerely,

ACKNOWLEDGMENT OF TERMS & AGREEMENT
Please indicate with your signature below that you have read the Assignment/Agreement letter and are in agreement with the guidelines and procedures set forth. Return a copy of this signed letter by mail or fax at this time.

_____   _____
Agent for Frederick Magazine   *Date*

Strategy Tip: *Be willing to go outside of your comfort zone in accepting writing assignments. Don't stretch it too far, though. I'd be willing to write technical marketing pieces or edit technical pieces, but writing a manual would be too far outside of my abilities.*

Rights

Contracts you sign with magazines will mention what rights the magazine is buying. Although they don't always use the same terms, you need to decipher what you are selling. You will find that most magazines will want to be the first to publish the article and also to be able to publish it electronically.

Once these actions are fulfilled, the rights revert back to you. Once the magazine publishes the article and puts it on their website, you are free to sell the article again as long as you don't try to sell first-time publication rights.

Here are some of the rights you will come across.

"First-run rights" or "Exclusive first rights" – This means the publisher owns the copyright on your text for a specified period of time, and during that time they will be the only one printing it. These rights can have other stipulations attached like "first-run rights for North America" or "first-run rights within the newspaper's distribution range." This last one is common for newspapers. If they give you money for a column, they understandably don't want you reselling that same column to a competitor, at least not until they've had a chance to print it first. You'd want "first-run rights" if you have a column that you're primarily selling to one newspaper to print first, with any number of "secondary" newspapers reprinting your articles afterward. In this case, the newspaper with first-run rights will pay more for your work than the other newspapers, as that paper is paying for the privilege of getting your work before anyone else.

"Full rights" or "All rights" – The publisher owns the copyright on the text, permanently. Once you give the newspaper your text, it becomes theirs, and you are no longer allowed to sell or print it without their permission.

"Reprint rights" – Your article may have already been printed somewhere else. "Reprint rights" or "one-time reprint rights" stipulate that you give permission for the article to be printed again, possibly in another form. A new publisher would need this permission from you before they can reprint a previously printed column.

Other restrictions or usages of your work –This could be a requirement that you won't sell the article to a competing newspaper within the same geographic range. It could be a stipulation that the paper reserves the right to archive your column, either in their personal archives or in a publicly available electronic archive.

These are important details that can determine what will happen to everything you give the publication. Make sure you understand every word in this contract.

Finally, retain your copyright! Sure, it's fine if the paper wants copyright and reprint rights for your article for a week/month/whatever, just as long as you eventually get the copyright back (that means, it's 100 percent yours again). From reselling to marketing to sentimentality, there are many reasons to maintain rights to what you write. For instance, I put a lot of my previously published stories and articles into book collections I publish, so I need to make sure the rights have reverted back to me.

Make sure you're not tied to a specific publisher for too long. Say, you have a falling out with a publisher, or your column takes off and you start to get requests for other papers or syndicates asking for your work. Who controls your articles? Like most things in life, leave yourself room to maneuver. The contract should say something like "publisher and freelancer reserve the right to terminate this agreement at any time" or "with one month notice" or a similar time frame. Stay away from any contract longer than a year, unless you have a good reason for doing so.

Prep Work

Once you get an assignment from an editor and accept it, you need to start the prep work.

Make yourself a list of specific people or types of people you need to interview for the article. Include the information that you will need to get from each of them. This will help you make sure you have all the essential information you need before you start writing.

I do all my research first, so I can get up to speed on a topic and not sound like a fool when I interview people. This also helps me develop interview questions.

With this initial information, I create a basic outline of how I want the story to flow. Since I haven't done interviews yet, I realize that this is a flexible outline.

Interviews

Part of your prep work will involve interviewing people. Readers want something more than they can find themselves with a casual search on the Internet. Interviews provide this because each interview can offer new information and perspectives on your topic.

Editors prefer to see quotes based on interviews you conduct rather than based on information published in existing works. Who or what you quote can vary depending on the type of article and the subject matter. For instance, with a history column, I may only quote historical sources, but in a history feature article, I will try to find historians or other appropriate sources I can quote in the article.

Interviewing someone might make you feel uneasy. Many writers are introverts, so stepping out of that comfort zone to not only have a conversation with a stranger but also be the one leading it can be hard to get used to. However, the more you do it, the more you will get used it. Also, you will become better at conducting interviews the more you do them.

I have to say that I have never been disappointed when I have taken the time to conduct an interview late in the writing process and then added those quotes to the story. Quotes add something to the story, whether it's new information, color, or credibility.

You should start thinking about who you will interview when you start planning your article. Start finding out how to contact these people. I make my initial contact for an interview via e-mail. It is not threatening, and it gives the person a chance to check out the publication where the article will appear. This allows them to consider whether they want to appear in that publication. If they don't respond within a few days, I will follow up with a phone call.

For smaller stories, stories on a short deadline, or interviews that are too far away to be cost effective, I conduct a phone interview. These are easy to do and often quicker than an in-person interview. However, you lose something by not talking to the interviewee face to face. The setting where the interview takes place and how the person dresses or acts can all contribute details to your story. Sometimes the interviewee has pictures, documents, or other items to show you. These can all add to your final story.

Phone interviews can work best for busy people. If I find someone is hesitant to be interviewed, I let him or her know that it will take only a certain amount of time (I base this on how many questions I have). I am also honest about the angle of the interview. I don't want the person feeling blindsided and complaining to my editor about obtaining an interview under false pretenses.

Once I have the interview set up, I write down a list of questions I want to have answered. I will research the topic and find out what holes in my information I need filled or what I might want to have someone elaborate on. I try to create questions that are open ended so the interviewee will need to give me more than a yes or no answer.

Understand that your questions should serve as a guide. If the interviewee answers with something you need explained or opens up with a new avenue of investigation, follow up. Your questions are a guide to bring you back on topic if the interview goes too far afield. It also lets you know when you have all the information you wanted to get and you can conclude the interview. A popular final question for interviews is "Is there anything you would like to add before we conclude?" It gives interviewees the opportunity to clarify anything they might think needs clarifying or it might even open up a whole new topic.

I like to record my interviews. I will let the interviewee know what I'm doing to make sure he or she has no objections. I have found that if I am only taking notes, not only can I get a quote wrong, but it can put a person on guard. They may talk more or less, depending on how they react to seeing you taking notes. If I am recording the interview, it becomes more like a friendly conversation between two people. It allows you to connect with the subject.

Remember that the interview is not about you. Keep things focused on the subject. You can mention yourself occasionally to make a connection with the interviewee, but keep it brief and get back to the interview. Don't start talking about yourself too much. Also, let the subject set the tone of the interview. He or she may want to be more formal, so there will be less joking and talking off topic.

Respond to the information the interviewee is giving you. Even if you don't need to follow up on an answer, saying "That's interesting" or "I hadn't considered that" lets the person know that you are paying attention to what he or she is saying.

However, you don't have to respond to everything the interviewee says. Sometimes silences will help you get needed information. Silences make people uncomfortable and they want to fill them. This means they may say a lot more than they intended.

Make sure when you write your article that you don't take a quote out of context or try to skew what the interviewee was trying to say. This can get you into trouble and ruin your reputation. I had a friend who used to joke about book blurbs because you couldn't necessarily tell if what was printed on the cover is actually about the book. His example was "… best book I ever read," but the full quote is "The best book I ever read was David Copperfield. This is not David Copperfield."

Some writers argue that you should leave in things like "uhs" or "umms" when writing out a person's quote. These are often used by a speaker when needing a pause in speech. They don't add to an interview most of the time, and using them in a quote can be distracting. An exception would be if the interviewee uses it for a longer pause or in place of an answer. Then it might be justified. However, I have seen writers use it to make the person sound like an idiot when that is not the case. This is the same as using a quote out of context.

The interviewee may ask to review the article when it is finished. This can be tricky. With newspaper articles, my answer is always "no." That is just the way newspapers operate. For a magazine article, though, I am more flexible. It can head off potential problems if you have a fact wrong.

If the story is a non-controversial feature, I'm more willing to let an interviewee review it to make sure I get things right. When I do, I always make sure to let the person know I am only looking for input on things that are factually wrong. I won't make changes that are about style or my interpretation of the subject matter because I am drawing my impressions from more than just the one person's interview.

If you are unsure of what to do, ask your editor. Let him or her make the final call.

When the interview is finished, make sure to thank the people for their time. You can also send an e-mail the next day thanking the interviewee. Ask your editor to send copies of the issue the story appears in to everyone you interviewed.

Titles

What is the first thing that will get a reader to stop and read an article? Pictures. But the second thing that will stop a reader is an interesting title.

You don't have control over the layout of your article unless you are publishing your own magazine, but you have some control over the title. It is just as important as a book title.

If you want to draw a further analogy between book titles and article titles, then article titles should be more like the title of a non-fiction book even to the point of using a subhead. Novel titles focus more on how words work together. *Jurassic Park, The Eye of the World, Demolition Angel*. They are good titles, but they don't tell you a lot of what the story is about.

Sometimes a magazine editor will use this type of headline, but he or she will always add a subtitle that describes the article's topic. Then your article title will become more like a non-fiction book title.

Non-fiction book titles need to be more descriptive. *Wheels for the World: Henry Ford, His Company, and a Century of Progress; The Devil in the White*

City: Murder, Magic and Madness at the Fair that Changed America and *Fallen Founder: The Life of Aaron Burr.* These types of titles are using the title as selling tool, whereas novels tend to sell the author.

Be aware, though, your editor may decide to change your article title. There's not a lot you can do about it since the editor is your client, and you want to make sure the client is happy.

Style

There are lots of ways to write an article. I certainly have my way, but that might not fit your style.

What I will say about writing articles is this: write something interesting that will hook readers. Usually the best way to do this is to write something that catches your attention. I believe that a writer's enthusiasm for the topic bleeds into his or her writing.

The first paragraph is the most important one in the article. It needs to grab the reader's attention right away whether you use a story, interesting fact, humor, or surprise as your hook.

Once you've got readers' attention, lead them into the main story with hard facts to give them a reason to continue reading.

Now build on what you've written. Add more details, quotes to support the story, and vignettes. This is one way to keep a reader interested, but so will provocative facts or surprises.

You'll need to strike a balance between using too much abstract language and too much detail. If you need to err, go with too much detail, which can be trimmed back later.

One final tip: Write in active voice. Try to paint pictures with words.

Types of Ledes

Since the first paragraph (called the lede in a newspaper article) sets the tone for the article, let's consider some of the more popular types of ledes.

- **Summary** – This is the type of lede old-school journalists were taught. It gives an overview of the subject, answering the basic questions for the reader (who, what, when, where, why, and how) in as succinct a manner as possible. Most of the time, it makes sense to focus on three or fewer of those questions to keep your opening tight.
- **Salient feature** – This lede puts the focus on one particular aspect of the story, giving emphasis to a single specific characteristic of the subject.
- **Case-approach** – This lede uses a specific story as a representative example to illustrate the point of the feature.
- **Suspense** – These ledes introduce the feature but cut off right before revealing the big

news of the piece. The effect is teasing the reader into perusing the rest of the story.

Since I often use the same lede for both my articles and query letters, you can see some examples of ledes in Appendix B: Sample Query Letters on page 211.

Subheads

Don't be afraid to use subheads in your article. It breaks up long blocks of text into easily digestible chunks. You won't see them used in newspaper articles often because most newspaper articles are relatively short. If you do see them, it will be in long features. If you are in doubt about whether to use subheads, check the magazine you are writing for to see if they are used in published articles.

Sidebars

As you write your article, you might find yourself with interesting or useful information that just doesn't fit within the article. Create a sidebar. Editors like them. It allows the text to be broken into smaller chunks, and it creates a graphic element for the layout. It also allows you to write a few hundred more words that you will be paid for.

Sidebars should be associated with the main story. It might be a list, personal experience, facts, quiz, where to find things in the story, useful tips, or something else related.

You don't need to format a sidebar when you write it, but you do need to indicate that section of copy is intended as a sidebar. I usually include mine at the end of the article. I write "SIDEBAR:" and then add the headline for the sidebar, followed by the copy. If the editor decides not to use it, it can easily be pulled.

Pictures

One advantage of magazines over newspapers is their layouts and graphics. They can help attract readers to your article, so think about possible things that aid in that endeavor.

If you can supply pictures to go along with your article, do so. If you are a decent photographer, take them yourself. You may even get paid extra if your pictures are used with the article.

Modern smartphones come with high-quality cameras. You can take pictures with your phone. You will want to study photos or learn about composition to improve your skills.

You will need to make sure the picture resolution is at least 300 dpi (dots per inch) in order for it to be publishable. You may see it listed as ppi (pixels per inch. Even if a picture looks fine on your computer screen, it may look pixelated in print.

How to check your photo dpi*:*

1. Right click on the photo file. You should see a list of options appear. The last one will be Properties.

2. Click on that and a box like the one on the next page appears.

3. Click on the Details tab. Under the Image section, you will see Horizontal Resolution and Vertical Resolution. Note that for this picture, the dpi is 600 dpi, so it is fine for publication.

If you do take your own pictures, make sure you get the names of anyone in the picture. At the very least, they will need to be identified in the photo caption. Some publications may also want you to have everyone sign a model release. Check with your editors for what, if anything, they require.

The larger a story you are writing and the more central to the issue it is, the more likely the editor will want to use their own photographer. Don't be offended.

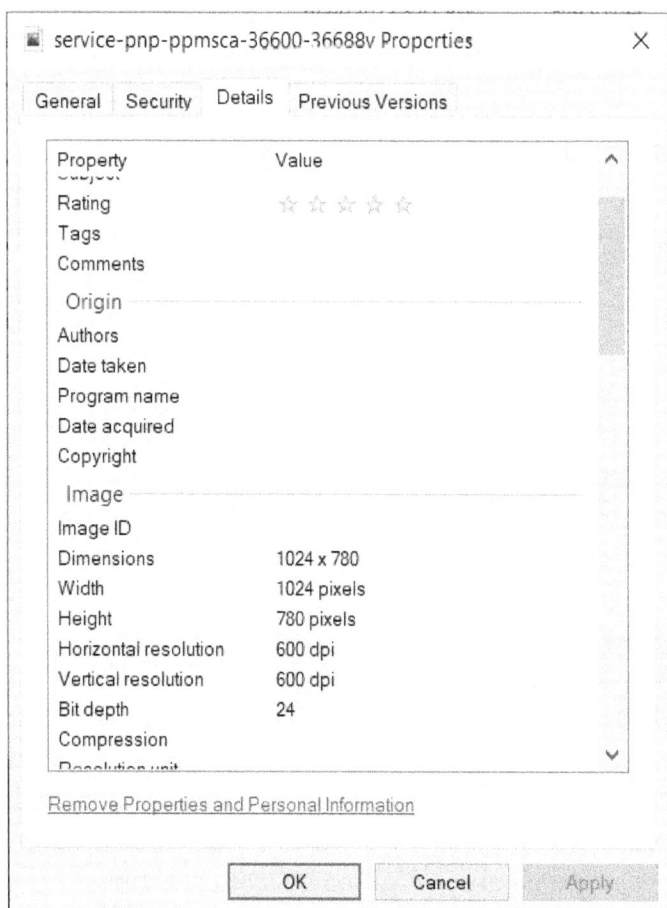

Newspapers

For the most part, newspapers should be approached the same way that you do magazines. Send a query letter to the editor of the section where you expect your article would appear (i.e., news, features, sports, columns, etc.)

The difference is that you will want to use the query letter to either pitch your own skills and experience to write for the newspaper as a stringer (an on-call writer) or to pitch a column idea. Newspapers, if they are looking for writers, aren't looking for someone to write just one article for them and be done. They want someone an editor can call on to fill in gaps staff writers can't cover.

The exception to this is when you are pitching a column. Then the editor wants to be convinced that it is a topic readers will be interested in and you are the best person to write it.

You may find that is actually harder to get newspaper assignments because newspapers tend not to use freelancers too often. That is why they have reporters. I think you will continue to see this trend as newsrooms continue shrinking. The opportunities for freelance writers will be as stringers. Editors will need them more to cover growing gaps in their coverage as the number of full-time reporters shrinks.

Don't expect stringing to pay well, though. From my own experience, if a publisher has both a newspaper and magazine, the magazine will undoubtedly pay two or three times what the newspaper pays for the same article, and newspaper-affiliated magazines tend not to pay as much as independent magazines.

The best place to try to break into newspaper writing is your local newspapers. You will be familiar with the stories the paper covers, what is going on in your area, and any gaps the newspaper has in its coverage.

Strategy Tip: *What sets a newspaper apart from its competition is local coverage. After all, most newspapers have the name of a city in their titles. Use this to your advantage and localize your pitch. I used to write a local history column for five different newspapers. The column title was the same, but the stories were localized to the paper it appeared in. It was more work, but it meant more sales.*

Rejection

Don't be surprised if you get a rejection letter in response to your query. Heck, don't be surprised if you get no response at all. I've probably gotten hundreds of rejection e-mails over the years. I suspect every author has gotten more of them than they would like.

It doesn't mean that you're a bad writer. The publication may have done something similar recently. The week before I wrote this section, an editor who asked me to write an article for his publication rejected two of my ideas. The magazine was planning for two similar articles in the issue before he wanted to run an article from me. Very bad timing on my part.

A rejection might also mean the publication doesn't want cover that topic.

You have to develop a thick skin. The best way I've learned to deal with rejection is not to dwell on it. When I was actively trying to get article assignments from magazines, I tried to send out at least a query letter each week and sometimes two.

If an editor passes on your idea (which might be a less harmful way of looking at it), write up a new query for the idea and send it to another editor. Don't dwell on the fact that an editor turned you down and let it keep you from writing and marketing.

This is one reason I tend to come up with the idea first and then try to find a market for it. If you have a story focused on getting published in one magazine, you may not have another market it can be submitted to if the editor passes on the idea.

Another way I dealt with rejection was I looked for the positive. When I first started sending out queries for short stories, I used to get form rejections that said, "Thank you for submitting your idea, but we are going to pass on this." Often they weren't even addressed to me. They would say something like "Dear Author." Then I noticed that editors started leaving a short note of encouragement at the bottom of the letter (back in the days when I submitted stories via snail mail). Then the letters became personalized to me or my query, and finally I started getting acceptances.

I used to keep a file of my rejection letters until I started wondering why. They were depressing even when I could see the progress I was making, so I finally threw the file out.

Along with rejection, you will have to deal with criticism. This can be a little more difficult because you need to address it.

You will have to learn to step back and examine what the editor or client is saying; it may be something that needs to be changed or corrected. Even if you feel you have a good case for not addressing the criticism, you can't ignore it. You should talk to the editor or client, explain your reasoning, and see if you can reach an agreement. If you can back up your position with more than "I like it that way," you have a chance at winning the exchange.

If the editor or client insists on having it done their way, then make the changes without grumbling about it. Remember they are the ones paying for your work. You need to make sure they get something they are happy with.

If the criticism is vague or you don't understand it, then ask questions until you do. You don't want to have to keep rewriting because it will be seen as your problem, not that the editor or client was vague.

Strategy Tip: *Keep track the queries you send and the responses from editors. You don't want to send the same pitch to the same editor. I recommend using a query tracking program. You will need it once you have a lot of queries circulating with different editors. I use Sonar 3. It's free and easy to use, but you can find others if you look around. A query tracking program will also let you see how long a query has been with a particular editor in case you want to do a follow-up to remind editors that you're still interested in writing for them. I usually wait at least two months.*

Meeting Deadlines

Your writing assignments will come with deadlines. Don't treat them lightly. If you miss deadlines, editors won't want to work with you.

Magazines and newspapers need to publish on certain dates. All the deadlines involved with publishing will work backwards from that point. There is some wiggle room built into the deadlines for unforeseen problems, but it is not your call whether you can take extra time to finish.

If you do run into a problem that will keep you from hitting your deadline, contact your editor as soon as possible and see what can be done. Even if there is a possibility of missing the deadline, give your editor a heads up. The editor might be able to help with whatever is keeping you from making the deadline. Otherwise, the editor can start making a Plan B to use if you do miss the deadline.

Most magazine editors will give you at least a month to complete your article. That sounds like a lot of time, but you'd be surprised at how quickly it can disappear when you've got other things that need to be done.

I've gotten into the habit of creating my own mini-deadlines. I will set a deadline for finishing interviews, first draft, and edits, so that I have a completed article by the deadline. If I'm juggling multiple articles, I prioritize the projects based on their deadlines, so that the article due first is the one I write first.

Do whatever works for you. Just make sure to meet your deadlines.

BUSINESS/
MARKETING
WRITING

Business writing can be articles in business-to-business publications, such as trade journals, but more commonly it involves creating ads, brochures, catalogs, and other marketing materials.

To know how to approach businesses about doing writing for them, you need to understand why a business might need help with writing,

While many businesspeople might be excellent in their work, they often lack confidence in their own ability to write. They are hesitant to admit it, but they can recognize good writing and feel they couldn't write to that level. It is understandable. Heck, a lot of professional writers feel that way.

Related to this is that businesspeople know their

limitations. They might feel they can write well, but they don't know how to put together a direct-mail package or structure an article. In this case, they need to tap into your expertise and experience.

They might lack the time to write. For them, it is a math problem. They can make more money doing what they do best compared to what it will cost to hire a writer.

Understanding what a businessperson's need is will help you target your approach to the business.

The most effective way to find business and marketing writing is to network through meetings of chambers of commerce, business associations, civic groups, and charitable work. Local professionals gather at these meetings, and you'll hear things about companies that need work.

Don't turn the meeting into a sales pitch for yourself, though. If you find a business needing writing services, say you might be able to help them and ask if you can call them about their needs.

Another way to make use of these meetings is to volunteer to be a speaker and talk about how businesses might improve their writing for sales letters or something that would appeal to a majority of those in attendance.

You will probably find your best success with local businesses because it is easy to maintain personal contact with the client.

It doesn't have to be local work, though. With

Zoom, phones, e-mails, and texting, it's easy to maintain contact with out-of-town clients.

Business writing is often writing copy for marketing materials, such as direct-mail packages, brochures, advertisements, newsletters, and annual reports.

One final place to begin searching is to put together a portfolio of your work and contact the local advertising, design, and public relations companies. I find design companies to be a particularly good source because they are designers not writers. If they have a project that requires writing, they either need to pass on it or get a freelance writer to help them.

It will take you more time to land these types of clients, but the relationships can last longer, provide more work, and pay better than many other types of business clients.

Pitching

The business-writing version of a query letter is the pitch. You will do two types of pitching for business writing.

If you want to write an article for a business publication or a trade publication that is only read by members of a particular industry, you approach them in the same way you do a magazine editor. Write a query letter. Structure it the same way you would for a consumer publication, but focus the idea on the business aspects for that industry. The best way to find out what will work for a business publication is to visit the publication's website or find some issues of the magazine. Then figure out if your story idea will work.

The problem you will run into is that many business publications don't have a website, or if they do, it is behind a paywall because professional groups often publish business publications. More than likely, you will find out about a publication by finding an older issue.

If you have some experience in a particular industry, you can pitch the editor to use you as a stringer who can write regular pieces for the magazine.

If you are interested in writing marketing pieces

for businesses, you will need to do a different type of pitching. You have to sell yourself as a copywriter (someone who writes marketing pieces).

Strategy Tip: *Some years back, I decided to digitize my pitch package. I now have a hidden webpage that is part of my website. It contains all the pitch package information and PDF downloads. When I pitch clients now, I will include a link to the page in my pitch letter to them.*

Research the business and find out who the proper contact is. You are generally going to be looking for the head of marketing, public relations, or communications.

Next, you need to prepare a package of information for that person. Begin with a pitch letter to sell yourself and your skills instead of a story. I encourage the person I am writing to to contact me for a project quote.

Then you want to have attachments to support that cover letter. I include a list of former clients sorted by industry, business articles, marketing samples, awards, client recommendations, and other honors.

Your pitch package is itself a demonstration of your ability to write marketing materials. It is essentially a direct-mail package selling yourself, so don't treat it lightly. If you can't sell yourself, marketing directors aren't likely to think you can sell their products.

Strategy Tip: *Some years back, I decided to digitize my pitch package. I now have a hidden webpage that is part of my website. It contains all the pitch package information and PDF downloads. When I pitch clients now, I will include a link to the page in my pitch letter to them.*

Project Quotes

Unlike magazines that usually list what they are willing to pay upfront, businesses will want you to quote a price. The two methods of quoting a price are by providing an hourly rate or a project rate.

The project rate is a single price for the entire project. An hourly quote is your hourly rate and it also includes an estimate of the number of hours. If you are working with a client who is demanding and will want a lot of changes or you are working in a field that you aren't familiar with, you may want to use an hourly rate. This can give you a buffer in case the project becomes more involved than you originally planned. If you can write quickly and efficiently, you can use a project quote. Businesses like this because they know up front how much it will cost. If you write quickly, then your hourly rate can be greater than if you actually quoted an hourly rate to the client.

Setting a rate can be hard to get right. That is why I prefer a project rate. I consider my experience in the field, how much research I need to do, the estimated time I think it will take, and how much I need to make to pay my expenses. I will then compare it to industry standards. My goal is that my rate is at the lower end of the industry range. (I like to use the Editorial Rates chart that the Editorial Freelancers Association publishes at www.the-efa.org/rates.) If it is higher, then I see if I can lower the quote. If I can't, then I usually don't expect to get the assignment.

Deciding on a rate can be almost an art form because I may lower rate expecting to get repeat work. Also, since there are only so many hours in the day, you need to find ways to work smarter. One way is getting multiple uses from your research and even your articles.

You will learn to get a feel for how long a project will the more projects you do. This will allow you to make better decisions about whether a project is actually worth your time. It may pay a lot, but if it takes longer than a typical project would, your hourly pay for the project might be less than a press release you can write in an hour.

Ad Tips

Having a salesman call on a customer can cost hundreds of dollars in expenses, time, and samples. A long-distance telephone sales call can cost up to $10. But an ad in a trade magazine can reach a prospect for about 50 cents.

In today's business marketplace where companies need to stay lean to stay competitive, effective business-to-business advertising is a must. This approach used to be called trade advertising, and while it can't actually close a sale for you, it can make the closing go much faster and smoother for the salesperson who calls on that customer.

For the most part, the same techniques that work for consumer ads work for business-to-business ads. However, understanding the audience you are addressing affects the way you use those techniques. Consumer ads are written for a general audience, while business-to-business ads are written for business owners and operators.

Here are some differences you should consider when you are writing business-to-business ads or other business marketing materials.

Testimonials – Testimonials can be an effective way to attract attention to your ad. However, in business-to-business advertising, it isn't Jennifer Lawrence or Jason Momoa who will attract a reader's attention. Instead, find an expert in the field to whom your product or service pertains: other scientists, businessmen, and technical experts. These are the people whose opinions matter to your audience.

Headlines – Catchy, slick headlines may work in consumer advertising, but with business-to-business ads, your headline must catch and hold the attention of someone who rarely has time to admire the word-smithing in a more commercial approach.

Many of today's copywriters seem to have abandoned the kind of writing that sells a client's product in favor of words that satisfy the writers' egos. An informational headline that promotes something new may seem boring, but for the company whose ad you are writing, it means money in the bank.

Body Copy – Make sure the body of the ad reinforces a benefit that is important to the customer. Give readers useful information, not hype. Don't generalize. Be specific and state the facts, figures, and sources that will enable customers to verify your claims if they have questions. Give customers the data they need to support their decisions with the people who have authority to sign the checks.

If the product requires a lot of copy to explain it, then write a lot of copy. You may think a product is boring, but a person who needs or uses it won't. The people who read your body copy are interested prospects. Don't let them off the hook by not giving them enough information to make a decision.

Demonstration – If you can devise a simple

demonstration readers can do on their own to compare your product with a competitor's, tell them how. Being able to see the results of a demonstration that they themselves perform can be a very effective selling tool, especially for technical people who are used to experimenting.

Positioning – Even if the product is considered an ordinary or common product in the industry, it can and should be differentiated in some way. The most successful commodity products come from those brands that are most successfully differentiated from the competition.

I once did this for a line of standardized laboratory chemicals by pointing out that the brand was the oldest brand in the industry, and it was sold to competitors under different labels.

Thus customers were paying higher prices for the exact same product.

The most common ways to differentiate commodity products are by lowest cost, best quality, or best service.

Closing – With business-to-business advertising, always include, at a *minimum,* a toll-free phone number customers can call for more information or to order. You want readers to be able to act on the immediacy created by reading the ad. Calling a phone number is the easiest approach. You should also consider adding a website.

Audience – Again, the one thing you must defi-

JAMES RADA JR.

nitely be aware of with business-to-business advertising is this: Whom are you talking to? In companies large and small, the people who use the products are often different from the people who authorize the product's purchase.

If this is the case with your product or service, you may want to consider creating separate campaigns for management and users. A campaign targeting users can follow the above guidelines, while a campaign for management should focus on the value your product or service will provide for the company.

With just a little adjustment in your thinking, you can move from writing excellent consumer ads to creating business-to-business ads that sell the products they promote.

Direct-Mail Tips

Most people think direct mail is junk mail. Yet mailboxes continue to be filled with everything from simple postcards to elaborate Publishers Clearing House–style packages.

Direct mail's appeal is that advertisers not only know exactly where all their sales come from, they know the effect of variables such as different pricing, premiums, larger or smaller packages, bill-later options, and credit card orders.

When writing a direct mail package, your primary job is to present the product in a way that gets readers over their aversion to doing business by mail.

- **Offer premiums to encourage greater response** – One of the most effective premiums is a contest or sweepstakes. I once wrote a package that included an entry into a drawing for $500 worth of free products from the sponsoring company. The response was a whopping 20 percent. However, while this method increases the response you receive, the people who respond often want only the gift or prize.

- **For more qualified customers, ask for full price or an up-front payment** – A three- to five-percent response is considered good, given today's cynical buyers. When you ask for up-front payments or full price, this figure drops, but the customers have greater product loyalty.

- **Use multiple pieces in your mailing** – A letter has one quick chance to hook readers, but a multi-piece package has many chances to catch readers' attention. Readers will usually look at each piece of a package before throwing it away. I once put together a subscription package that included a letter, a teaser letter, a brochure, and a reply card. All of them contained a selling message. That gave me four chances to hook the reader.

- **Generate leads with initial low-cost mailings you can follow up** – My personal direct-mail package used to include a letter and reply card. If readers wanted more information, they mailed the cards back. The package costs me about 60 cents to print and mail. For that amount, I receive about a five- to six-percent response that I then follow up with a more expensive package. Nowadays, I do this online and save money, but the response rate stays about the same.

• **Enclose a stamped reply card to make it simple to respond** – This gives customers a no-cost way to reply. Include another selling message on the card. Also, having a buyer's signature on the card protects you if a buyer decides to dispute a credit card charge.

• **Omit the return address on the outside envelope** – This helps create curiosity so readers don't throw the envelope away without opening it. I've never used this method, but I know it works on me. I'm reluctant to throw something away when I don't know who sent it.

• **Use teasers to encourage readers to open the envelope** – Ask a question and offer the answer inside: "Win $500 worth of ACME products… plus, get a FREE T-shirt. Details inside."

• **Personalize your letters** – Computer programs and e-mail management websites like Mailchimp and Mailerlite allow you to select demographic characteristics and easily drop in a name in appropriate spots. Another way to personalize letters is to put computer-generated, "hand-written" comments on the letters. An example could be an arrow drawn in colored ink pointing to the offer in the letter. The margin note could say something like, "Wow! This offer saves you $1,000!"

- **Hook a prospect in the first ten words** – If you don't, the package will more than likely go into the trash. Sell fast and hard. Many people don't like a hard sell, but because you can't be with readers in person to see how to best sell the product, you need to blast with both barrels.

- **Start with something important to the reader** – For instance, tell prospects they will "Save hundreds of dollars in interest payments," rather than say, "Bank X's credit card only charges 2% APR."

- **Ask your customers to respond immediately** – If you set a deadline for obtaining the premium, readers will be more likely to act quickly. As a general rule, you'll get about 80 percent of your responses in the first two weeks after you send out a direct-mail piece.

- **Stress an additional sales point in your P.S.** – Studies have shown that the postscript is one of the most read parts of a letter. Make it sell! For example: "If you're still unsure Black Issues in Higher Education is for you, try our eight-month trial subscription for just $18. Check the 'Maybe' box on the reply card and mail it back. It's an offer you can't afford to pass up and a magazine you can't afford to miss."

- **Make the reply card easy to fill out when ordering** – Don't risk frustrating readers. Ask for a customer's name, address, and method of payment (now, bill me, credit card). If you're accepting credit-card orders, you also need to ask for the credit card type, expiration date, CVV code, and number, as well as get the customer's signature.

• **Make sure your mailing list targets people who would be interested in your product** – The more precise you can make your list, the better your response will be. In my mailings, I use different letters. My general letter pulls about a five percent response, while my letter targeted to biotech firms pulled three times that amount because the letter addressed the specific questions of biotech firms.

• **Once you have a successful mailing, use it as a control** – Alter different variables, such as price, offer, and premiums to try to create mailings that pull better than your control. This process of reevaluation will help make your mailings more cost effective and more successful.

SCIENTIFIC/ SCHOLARLY WRITING

Scientific and scholarly writing is the hardest market to break into as a freelance writer. It has a steep learning curve because it can be highly technical writing that is footnoted and often peer reviewed. You also tend to need specialized knowledge to write well in the field.

Manuals and technical guides will pay very well, but scholarly and scientific articles usually don't pay at all. This is because most of the articles are written by scientists who write them as a way to build their credentials in the field.

Freelancers are more likely to make money from scholarly articles by working as an editor for a scientist. While scientists and engineers want to build their credentials, they are reluctant to write.

Frank R. Smith, a former editor of *Technical Communication,* a journal of the Society for Technical Communication, said in an article in *The Editorial Eye* that of the many papers he read each year for possible publication, "most are written by the same people." Bill French, a former executive director of the American Society for Photogrammetry and Remote Sensing, agreed, adding in the same article, "It's a constant battle to find practical papers."

Harvey Bjelland, in his book *Writing Better Technical Articles,* wrote, "In science, agriculture, bacteriology, chemistry, forestry, engineering, mining, medicine, metallurgy, physics, or any other technical field, writing is essential in most stages of every important project if a person does not wish to remain anonymous." Though the publish-to-survive mandate is a part of academic life that many regret, Smith said that "publishing an article is like getting an endorsement from an outside authority. It's a positive factor when a [performance] review comes up."

Christina Kessler, former editor of the *Construction Specifier,* agreed. She told *The Editorial Eye* that "writing articles builds credentials."

Kessler said of engineer-writers, "Their style is a little dry, but their English is no worse than anyone else's." But most technical people know that they need to learn to write better. French said engineers don't know how to write because their education was heavily based in science rather than liberal arts. Tim Reason, former assistant editor for the *Professional Surveyor,* believes there's a lesson to be learned from technical people without degrees. "We are occasionally disappointed with articles received from academics. Surveyors are not so self-conscious about writing. They like airing issues."

Despite having everything to gain professionally by publishing an article, most engineers say they don't have the time or don't think they have anything to write about. The first problem can be solved by emphasizing the benefits of having an article published: Writing is the only tangible result of much engineering research. The second problem can be solved by gaining a wider perspective: Because they do it day after day, engineers may fail to see their work as unique.

Bjelland suggested a third reason for not writing: fear of being seen as inexperienced or not knowledgeable. This can be solved by striving for excellence in writing as just one more aspect of research: The profession can't advance if technical people don't write about their work.

> **Strategy Tip:** *If you want to try to make money from scientific and scholarly writing, try ghost-writing articles. Scholars may not be open to this because they feel they can write well, but scientists often don't enjoy writing. They may be open to hiring a ghostwriter.*

Getting Started

The easiest way to get your foot in the door in this field is to network and meet people in companies that are looking for writing help. Offer them a low rate for the work initially, so you can gain experience. Don't mention that as the reason for the low price, though. It might make them reluctant to use your services if they think of you as a beginner.

If you have a particular scientific or engineering skill that will help you get started, focus on those companies where that experience is relevant. Approach the companies as you would if you were seeking marketing work at a business.

A variation on this is to come in through the marketing side of the business. I was amazed at how much I learned writing marketing materials for a biotech company. Before too long, I understood a lot of the basics of the technology and could successfully work with scientists on manuals and guides.

Technical writers come in two types: ones with scientific backgrounds and ones with writing backgrounds. Starting out, both types are at a disadvantage in delivering well-written technical materials. The former's writing may not have style or communicate well, and the latter's writing may talk down to the reader or lack scientific underpinnings.

They aren't technical writers yet. That title comes with experience. True technical writers have a fundamental understanding of science and an ability to convey information in an effective way to a scientific audience.

When I started technical writing, my experience was as an advertising copywriter. I knew that I needed a better understanding of biotechnology (the industry I was writing about), but how could I get that understanding without going back to school?

I got a job with the marketing communications department of the biotechnology company.

This is a great way to get a scientific education in any scientific field. Marketing writers create ads, brochures, catalog copy, and direct mail campaigns. The emphasis isn't so much on the science but the selling.

That doesn't mean you don't need to know the science behind the products. Marketing writers meet with technical experts to get a basic understanding of the products or procedures being marketed.

Outside of the basic marketing meetings, I also took time to watch the products in use in the laboratory. Then I would meet with the marketing director for the product and ask questions about details that might not wind up in the copy but would further my understanding of how customers used the products and for what purposes.

As you gain more industry-specific knowledge, you will be trusted to work on materials that require a greater scientific understanding, such as sell sheets, articles, and manuals. These materials require meetings with scientific experts and marketing managers, but the discussions follow a more scientific style.

Throughout all of this, you should take advantage of learning opportunities that come your way. This might be taking classes offered by your company or simply studying the comments made by technical experts on your copy.

I soon learned to talk to technical experts in a manner they could relate to, and I gained an understanding of how the products worked and could ask better questions about them.

When I decided to strike out on my own as a freelancer, I had two years of technical-writing experience under my belt and lots of samples that I could use to demonstrate my ability. More importantly, I had lots of contacts with people I had met who worked with other companies and former employees of the company I was leaving.

My first freelance work was with biotechnology companies because that is where my scientific knowledge was based. However, when someone I knew went to work at a technical journal, she hired me to be a freelance copyeditor. This turned out to be another learning experience for me. To do the copyediting, I had to read the articles, and I was soon gaining a wider understanding of molecular biology. This allowed me to work as a freelance editor with some technical experts to help them prepare their articles.

I believe that most writers can become effective technical writers if they are curious. The key is wanting to understand new things and being willing to ask questions. It may take some people a little longer to gain an understanding, but as long as you are interested and show that interest, most technical experts will respond to that interest with patience and a willingness to explain things to you.

Working with Technical People

The most important thing to understand about technical experts is how much their work matters to them. Writing related to that work must often be done on a tight deadline, because this step usually occurs at the very end of a lengthy stint of careful research. Career advancement for scientists and other technical people may depend on how well their writings are received. Their reluctance to relinquish control over their projects to someone who might harm their standing is only natural. This issue is the root of much of the tension you may feel when beginning to work with any technical expert.

Here are some guidelines for minimizing the conflict inherent in your position.

1. Before you start a writing project, hold a planning meeting – I like to meet with anyone who has a say in the approval of my final product. That way, I know before I start working what everyone who could delay approval expects from me, and I can resolve potentially conflicting opinions from the beginning.

Review information on the project beforehand so you can ask incisive questions. Then get the experts talking about their research project and keep them talking. Use the dialogue to confirm or correct your preliminary analysis of the objectives, unique aspects, and implications for other areas of the research you will be writing about: show early on that you are aware of the critical areas.

State your intention to make the technical people look as good as possible in print. Tell them that you are not trying to change the results of the original research, but rather to make it easier for others to read about and replicate.

Set the parameters of your respective roles. A scientist may think you are there "only" to edit when you have been asked to write. Are you a technical writer, a copywriter, or a copyeditor for a particular project? Get it spelled out. Make sure that everyone involved agrees on the division of tasks. A scientist who had written a laboratory guide once thought I was using it as marketing copy when, in fact, the project manager had told me to copyedit it. The scientist was stunned when he saw my revised version of his cherished guide.

2. Get technical experts to approve an outline – Preparing an outline is usually the first thing I do after the planning meeting, when what we've agreed on is fresh in my mind and everyone is geared up to move ahead. Some technical experts will reject anything you write simply because they didn't write it, but if you already have their approval on a preliminary outline, they are less likely to reject subsequent drafts. You can send a copy of your outline to any players who were unable to make it to the planning meeting. This isn't foolproof, but in conjunction with consulting with experts as part of the writing process, it helps.

3. Assess each expert's need for involvement – The personalities you'll encounter range from those who don't want to be bothered with writing up last month's research to those who doubt that anyone outside their team is competent to write up their work. Become attuned to these variations in temperament and accommodate them. They tell you how much control you will actually have over the project. When I ask for preferences, I commonly hear both "Whatever you think is best" and "I've published a dozen papers. I know what scientists want to hear."

Experts who say they don't want to be involved in the writing at all are asking for inaccuracies in the final product, so you must insist on at least minor participation, for both your sakes. Those who review but reject everything you write will eventually have to settle for something. A third party may have to be called in to arbitrate. When I worked for the marketing department of a biotechnology company, the project manager, who it happened was neither a writer nor a researcher, would settle disagreements or stalemates between the technical expert and me.

4. Don't run to the experts with everything – Select with care the issues you present to them for comment, or you may be courting further controversy. Be a quick study. Find textbooks or other outside sources you can go to for answers.

5. Be patient – While your job is getting a project completed, a technical expert's job is developing new products. When a project is taken out of the hands of the technical experts and given to you, they won't simply sit around waiting. If it comes to them while they are engaged in an intense phase of their new project, your draft may be set aside. Write a "need by" date on each draft and leave people alone until that date has passed. You may have to ask a higher-up to intercede for you with habitual foot-draggers whose advice you need.

6. Be as diplomatic as you can when you revise

anything – Make positive comments as well as correc-
tions. Mention passages that read particularly well, and
make it clear that you are trying to preserve the integri-
ty of important passages by asking for assistance.

Give hard facts, not opinion. For example, instead
of "I don't think the DNA strand can be sliced between the two target genes," say "An article in *Bio-
techniques* 35:4 said that scientists haven't been able
to isolate one of the target genes you've mentioned.
Can the DNA still be sliced if the gene can't be iso-
lated?" Give the technical experts enough information
to make a correct reply so that you in turn can improve the writing.

List all the authors for source material when you
prepare the references for cited material. This is not a
fine point. To the technical community, inclusion in a
bibliography verifies a contribution, but often space
allows the listing of only the lead authors and the rest
must be lumped under et al. Fight for listing everyone. The last thing you want to do is alienate potential
users of your method or product, and the technical
community is a pool of potential users.

Manual-Writing Tips

While creating user-friendly manuals would seem
to be an obvious step in product development, it is
one that is frequently forgotten. This oversight does
not mean that the authors don't know their products.

Although technical writers may know what chemicals to pipette into what test tube, they often draw a blank when they try to put what they know on paper.

Writing manuals is a time-consuming process that you can make easier or harder on yourself. If you approach the task with enthusiasm, it will carry over into your writing and help you write a manual that won't put readers to sleep or set their teeth on edge with frustration. Look at manual writing as tying all the product-development efforts together in a friendly way that makes the product that much more attractive to a user. Your readers will appreciate your hard work, and they'll show it by continuing to buy the product.

Here are five suggestions for making documentation as painless as possible for both you and your readers.

1. Keep your language simple – This basic rule for all types of writing is consistently ignored. Keep in mind that you are writing to offer information to someone else, not to impress the user with how much technical knowledge you have. Having someone unfamiliar with the product try to follow the procedures (which some research scientists call protocols) that you've written in an early draft of the manual is a good way to see how well you are communicating. If this reader can't follow the procedures, you need to rewrite them.

Here are two ways to keep the writing clear and simple:

Use the second person wherever possible. Some clients may insist that second person is too informal, but tell them it's the quickest way to get readers' attention and the surest way to move them from A to B.

Avoid passive voice and smothered verbs. They make sentences longer and insulate the meaning from the reader. (See the example in rule 2.)

2. Tell readers why they should read the manual – At the beginning, you should always have some sort of introductory paragraph or overview that answers the question, "What's in this for me?" An overview not only tells the reader what to expect from the manual, but it also serves as a map for you as you write-tell what you need to say to accomplish the objectives you set.

Here's the opening line in the overview of a manual I edited: "The System for In Vitro Expression of peR Products is designed to permit the preparation of peR products that can rapidly be transcribed, translated, and cloned."

This sentence, despite the long kit name, does say what the product will do for the reader. There's a problem, though: The statement contains two passive constructions (is designed, can be transcribed...) and a smothered verb (preparation). The publisher and the user are invisible and it is less than clear exactly what the user can do. This rewrite is better: "The System... allows you to prepare peR products for rapid transcribing, translating, and cloning."

3. Assume that your readers are novices – This is important from the very beginning. Don't take the chance that you will be writing over someone's head. Readers who are experts will most likely skip over the overview; those who read it are often unfamiliar with the product.

Also, the easiest way to lose a reader is by using acronyms that haven't been spelled out. While this doesn't include such basic scientific terms as DNA and RNA, it does include the more advanced acronyms. How do you decide what's "advanced"? Consider the audience. For example, a cell culturist knows that IVD stands for in vitro diagnostic, but a molecular biologist may not.

Conversely, don't talk down to your readers. Nothing insults them more than realizing that the writer thinks of them as idiots. Here's an example I caught in the first draft of a manual I edited: "The milky-white plaques are small, of low contrast, and easily missed by novice BEVS practitioners."

Most professionals do not particularly enjoy being called novices, and writers who make such offhand references can seem condescending. This sentence was easily fixed by deleting "by novice BEVS practitioners."

4. Be thorough in the methods section of the manual – This is the critical section. Assume that your reader has never performed the procedure before. The ease with which a reader can use the procedurcs you outlinc will makc or brcak thc product. Don't risk a dissatisfied customer because you wrongly assumed that the intermediate step between 1 and 2 was too obvious to mention. There are two important offshoots of this rule.

Omitting information confuses readers. Consider this step if you saw it in a manual: "Centrifuge the appropriate volume of suspension culture for the number of cells necessary for the experiment."

The information needed to perform the step was left out because the writer was so familiar with the product that he or she took for granted that the user would know what the relative centrifugal force should be. What's the centrifugal force? For how long do you centrifuge the sample? Here's a more specific way to say it: "Use the appropriate volume of suspension culture for the number of cells necessary for the experiment. Centrifuge the culture at 12,000 x g for 5 minutes."

Make sure you place steps in the right order. If the reader is performing the experiment or process step-by-step, placing the steps out of order ·could cause an experiment or procedure to fail. Placing two actions out of order in the same step could also cause failure. Here is an example of a common error I run into when I am editing manuals: "Discard the supernatant and keep the pellet."

If directions are followed as written, the reader will not be able to keep the pellet because it will have been discarded with the supernatant. Though a writer may find it hard to believe that someone would read only half a step, perform it, then read the second half of the step and try to perform it, believe me, it happens every day. Technical services departments are always getting calls for help in cases like this.

5. Tell your reader all the ways the final product can be used – Don't be afraid to brag about the many uses for your product. More uses mean a larger audience of possible users and more perceived value for your product. Besides, no one knows your product as well as you do, so if you don't tell your readers how to use it, who will?

Getting Technical Writing Right

Just as chemical elements make up different compounds, good technical writing—whether an instruction manual, a technical article, or product data sheet—has six traits in common.

It's correct: Since most technical writing tends to instruct in some way, accuracy is critical. A technical mistake can ruin an experiment and make the results unobtainable for your reader. For instance, if a test kit is supposed to be stored at -200 C and you write "Store components at 200 C," the reagents in the kit will be ruined.

Some technical writers may think that because this mistake is a so-called typo; it's not their responsibility.

Wrong! This is the type of error that many editors wouldn't catch or even check. They would assume that you knew at what temperature to store the kit. If your writing has too many careless errors, you will lose your credibility with knowledgeable readers and, eventually, with your editors or clients.

It's consistent – Consistency makes your writing look professional. While in many cases the effect is subtle, referring to processes or pieces of equipment in the same way each time drives home your message more clearly than if you call something by three different names.

Here's how inconsistency can confuse readers. In a manual I edited, a procedure recommended the use of a medium called "Sf-900 II SFM." Related procedures referred to the medium as "SF-900 II" and "Sf-900." Cell culturists use "Sf" as an abbreviation for an insect line and "SF" as an acronym meaning "serum free." Also, "Sf-900 II SFM" is an improved medium. By omitting the generation number, the scientist left readers wondering if he really meant for the first-generation medium to be used.

It's clear – Much technical writing tends to be involved and complicated. Yet, many of the complications come from the writing itself rather than the subject matter. Procedures should be described with such precision that a reader can easily and accurately perform the same procedure. How can readers duplicate your results if your findings are buried in abstract nouns, puzzling antecedents, and passive verbs? The greater the success readers have with your procedures, the greater your credibility will be.

I edited a manual in which one step of a procedure read, "Heat the mixture to 650 C, then chill for 2 min." Heat at 650 degrees for how long? What is the exact temperature for "chill"? There is no way a reader can accurately duplicate this step. Later, a corrected version of this sentence read, "Heat the mixture to 650 C for 10 min., then chill on ice for 2 min."

It's concise – All readers appreciate tightly written copy because it's easier to understand and gets to the point quickly. Just the sight of a long manual or article can be intimidating. Wordy procedural steps and explanations tend to result when writers want to sound intelligent and knowledgeable but aren't sure they will. Which of the following examples do you prefer? "An insatiable need to know that which it did not understand led to the inevitable demise of the felis catus," or "Curiosity killed the cat."

Though this is a facetious example, technical literature is filled with instances of writers filling up pages rather than informing readers. Using active voice and imperative forms will help cut down the word count. Instead of writing "The program shall be tested," write "Test the program." Instead of writing "Latex gloves should be worn by the user," write "Users should wear latex gloves," or "Wear latex gloves." The "you" understood in the imperative is clearer and involves the reader more directly than does any abstract noun.

It's convincing – Your primary goal as a writer is to tell readers about a better way to do something. While your method or idea may give better or faster results, readers aren't necessarily going to adopt it. Inertia keeps things moving on the same path unless there is a compelling reason for them to change direction. To get readers to change direction, you must persuade them that your ideas are better. Explain how your results relate to your readers' work and can improve their performance. Highlight the selling points.

The overview of a manual I edited stated, "The RACE procedure amplifies and clones rare mRNAs and may be applied to existing cDNA libraries. Additionally, products of the RACE reaction are directly sequenced without any intermediate cloning steps, or the products may be used to prepare probes."

This is only the first of many places where the author touted his kit's strongest selling points, helping to convince readers of the value of his method.

It's catchy – Technical writing has a reputation for being dry and boring, and much of it is. But if you bore your readers across the board, they may never finish the article. You want readers to walk away feeling positive about your method and interested in trying it. Lively copy can be achieved through the use of short sentences, a friendly style, and, in some cases, even humor.

If you want to write outstanding technical pieces, you shouldn't try to sound like everyone else. These six elements will start you on your way to writing technical articles, manuals, and data sheets that will catch readers' attention and keep them reading.

Some examples of scholarly and scientific writing where my articles have appeared. These types of articles might be peer reviewed, heavily footnoted, and less dramatic in their style. They might also include technical editing, such as the manual seen at the lower-right corner.

Breaking Through Writer's Block

Sooner or later, you'll run into writer's block. You won't or can't write. It's frustrating, but know that every writer has encountered it in some form even if they don't want to admit it.

The obvious symptom of writer's block is that your work isn't getting done. You procrastinate. If you do this too long, it can cause you to miss deadlines.

The most likely reason for writer's block is the nature of the work that we do as writers. It can be very personal and emotional, particularly when we write fiction. You have to open yourself up to write authentically, and that can be stressful.

Don't let it scare you, and most importantly, don't let it control you.

Write daily – The first cure is scientific. Newton's First Law of Motion tells us that an object in motion tends to remain in motion, so write every day.

If you are used to writing every day, then stopping will be hard. You will have developed the habit of writing, and your body and mind will expect to write daily. It also helps if you can write at the same time each day, but this might be pushing it.

Multiple projects – That said, you don't have to write daily on the same project. A technique I use that has helped me avoid writer's block is that I am always working on multiple projects at the same time. If I get stuck on one project, I'll jump to working on another one and come back to the original project at another time. At the time I am writing this book, I have just launched a novel, I have another book in layout, and I'm writing the draft of a fourth book. I am also working on probably a dozen different articles. Something to keep in mind if you find yourself doing this is that while it keeps you writing, it can indicate you are bored with a project. It might be time to look at the project and see if it is actually working. I know when I am excited about a project, I can get lost in it and spend too much time working on it to the detriment of my other projects.

Write through it – I had a newspaper editor give me advice that is useful for a third technique. Don't try to get it perfect. Just write through it. If you run into a spot that you can't figure out what to write, write a note about what you need in the spot and then jump to the next point where you know what you want to write. You can come back and fill in gaps on your ncxt draft.

Set personal deadlines – This one can be a double-edged sword. Yes, deadlines put pressure on you to get writing done, but maybe, you are putting too much pressure on yourself. If you have set a daily word count, maybe you've set it too high for what works with your overall schedule. While it might work for another writer, you need to find what works best for you.

These techniques assume the problem is you. If the problem is the story itself, you've got some work to do.

The way I deal with this is that I outline what I have written and compare it to the outline to look at the changes and decide if the changes should stay or if I should move in a different direction. I have done both. I have rewritten sections to bring it back in line with the original outline, and I have made changes to the outline based on what I've written.

The biggest change I've ever made was when I was writing my historical novel, *Canawlers*. I was about halfway through the draft when I ran up against a wall. I couldn't work through it, so I outlined what I had written so far. Then I started moving scenes around. Finally, I decided that the best way to move forward was to kill off one of my main characters who had still been alive at the end of the original outline.

Indie Publishing

Rather than write for a client who will then publish what you write and pay you for it, e-publishing is publishing digitally, and it is the easiest way to get started in indie publishing. You can do it yourself.

It is an inexpensive way for you to reach people directly with your writing and have those readers pay you based on how well you write.

The three major types of e-publishing you will find are: blogs, e-zines, and e-books.

Blogs

Think of a blog as a list of published articles on a particular topic. Blogs aren't as popular as they once were, but they are still out there, and if you can find an audience, a blog can be profitable.

Your best chance of having a successful blog is to write on a topic where you can define the audience. The more specific it is, the better. So don't just write about history, write about American history, or better yet, the history of your state.

The articles are called posts, and they are generally just a few hundred words long. However, posts can also contain pictures, videos, and links. These are all additional ways to engage your readers.

Blogs can be monetized with ads on the same page. If reader click on the ad, they are taken to the ad sponsor's website. If a purchase is then made, you will get a percentage of the purchase.

You can also do something similar with your own links in the posts. You do this by joining an affiliate program for a particular product or company. The program will create the links you need that are coded so that you will receive a percentage.

A variation on this is to turn the monetization over to a third party who will place various ads and links on your blog. You then get paid by how many readers either click on the links or view the posts.

And finally, you can sell your own products direct to readers through links and ads in your posts. This will be the most profitable way for you to earn money because you keep a greater percentage of the sale.

Earning a decent amount of money from a blog can be difficult. You either need to develop a large audience or a very specific audience who will be interested in your products as well as your writing.

You also need to write posts for your blog regularly. Most people try to update their blogs a couple times a wcck. Each timc you put a new post up, you give readers a new reason to visit the blog and perhaps make a purchase.

WordPress is a popular platform for blogs. It is also a nice feature that you can tie into a website that is built on WordPress. This will give people a reason to visit your website regularly.

E-ziŋes

E-zines are a step above blogs. They are set up more like a magazine, which means they might have columns and letters from readers and other elements from a magazine. However, the articles will often look like a blog post.

E-zines will also have ads and links like a blog that create additional streams of revenue.

However, an e-zine won't publish as often as a blog. Also, rather than publishing a post at a time, e-zines are published as a magazine would be with a block of articles.

Some magazines are published on e-book platforms so they are actually more formatted and tend to look fancier than a regular e-zine.

Although there may be some blogs that have paid subscribers, I haven't found any. However, there are e-zines that have paid subscribers.

I have written for some e-zines, but I have not published one. The closest I've come is publishing the two newsletters that I send to my followers monthly. Currently, I don't want to have to do an e-zine where I will have to meet another deadline every month.

E-books

E-books are generally considered electronic editions of novels and non-fiction books. However, e-books can include novellas and short stories. Kindle has even introduced Vella, a publishing format for a serial story.

I enjoy selling e-books, and they make up a large part of my income each month. The big advantage is that once you publish an e-book, it can continue to earn you money month after month, year after year.

You need to continue publishing additional books and not rely on a single book for regular income. The larger your library of titles grow, the larger your income will grow each month, generally.

I continue to experiment with e-books, trying different price points, different types of books, and different forms of marketing. I continue with what works and tweak what doesn't to try to make it better.

I've done e-book only and e-book versions of my existing print novels. I've also done short fiction. I have found that it is easy to publish an e-book and that I don't really need a publisher working as a middleman.

The nice feature of e-publishing is that it is scalable. Once you have a book, you can market it and sell it over and over. You can publish is as an audiobook and physical book. You can turn it into stories, a series, or create associated materials. These all build your sales and increase your income from one product. Now add a second product and a third.

A display at a bookstore of some of the books I have indie published. Most of these books also have e-book editions. Indie book publishing has become an attractive alternative for many authors.

Why Indie Publish?

Whenever there is a recession, book buying at the large publishing houses tends to dry up. Over the years, a lot of medium-sized publishers have also been gobbled up by the large publishers. This means that the chances of you winning a publishing deal from a publisher shrink.

However, this also creates an opportunity for smaller publishers, in particular indie publishers. I'm a big fan of indie publishing. Here's why:

You can keep your book in print – The average book remains in print a year. For a new author, it may be hard to stand out from the thousands of books that are published in a month. When I started indie publishing, I only made a few hundred dollars in my first month. However, I kept at it, publishing more books, marketing the ones I was publishing, building my platform, and getting better at my craft. Because of that, my income continues to grow. My earliest e-books are still in print while my first novels that were published with mainstream publishers are long out of print. Well, actually, I got the rights back, and I have republished one as an e-book already.

You can make more money – I make about ten times for each of my physical books sold than what a traditionally published author makes. For e-books, I make about twice as much. That can vary based on how I sell the book. My first novel was traditionally published. It sold around 10,000 copies in paperback and audio, and for that, I made less than $5,000 over three years for a book that retailed at $9.95. Nowadays, I can sell at least 1,000 paperback and e-books of a new title in the first year. It will probably earn me around $10,000.

You can attract a major publishing house – Large publishers are watching for indie books that sell well. It shows them that the author has a platform and is willing to market the book. You become a proven quantity, and they are more willing to invest in that.

Christopher Paolini self-published his novel *Eragon* when he was fifteen years old. It sold thousands of copies before it captured the attention of a New York editor. That book became a quartet of novels and a movie.

You can get your book to market faster – With a traditionally published book, it will take you at least a year after signing the contract to see your book on the shelves. That doesn't include how long it takes you find a publisher who says "yes" once you write it. If your book is about a timely topic or trying to capitalize on a trend, it is likely to miss the optimum time to hit the market.

As an indie publisher, you can have your book on the market within a couple months after it is fully edited and ready for publication.

You maintain the control of your book – You might not think this is a big deal as long as you get paid, but I have known authors who had publishing houses change their story or leave in mistakes that the author asked to be corrected. I had a publisher change the title of one of my books. I also had a story rejected because it had to be a unanimous decision by the publisher's committee and one person had a "factual" problem with the story, and my facts were correct, which I showed the committee. However, the person wouldn't change her mind and so the story wasn't published.

Write It, Edit It

Indie publishing is not for books that can't get published. A bad book is a bad book. So the first thing you need to do as an indie publisher is write the best book you can.

Some people will tell you to write to a niche or a genre. Others will tell you to write to market (write a book about whatever the hot topic is).

They're all right, and they're all wrong. For instance, those who talk about writing to market are thinking more as a businessperson. The same can be said about writing in a specific genre to a certain extent.

And that's fine. It works for them. However, I write because I love writing, and I particularly love writing the stories I want write. I write both fiction and non-fiction. I also write in a variety of genres. I do this because those are the stories I want to tell.

I don't write to market because often what's hot isn't a type of story I want to write. However, I do look at what is hot among my own books, and I have been known to move a project up that is part of a series or genre that is doing well for me. I do this because I know I can get strong sales from a new title, and the income will help fund new projects.

I also write books that I want to write because they are easier for me to sell. I am interested in them, and when I talk about them, people can hear me get excited. I am pretty sure this wouldn't be the case if I was writing to market. I can't see myself getting excited about a topic I wrote only because I thought it would sell well.

I publish fiction and now non-fiction because they are the projects I love. I figure if I still love the project after it's done, then I will be a better salesperson because of it, and since I'm not a natural salesperson, I need all the help I can get.

Once you have written the book you love, you need to step back and allow an editor to go over it. By the time you've read your manuscript a few times, your eyes will not register some mistakes.

An editor has fresh eyes and will catch those errors and make recommendations on the story itself. There are different types of editors, a developmental editor will work with you to improve the story while a copyeditor will simply correct grammar and spelling.

You can find editors in writing magazines, on the Internet, and through various writing organizations. You can also ask for referrals from other writers, particularly those who write in your genre.

Contact the editor and ask for references and

books they have edited. Make sure the editor is familiar with your genre.

Talk to the editor and make sure you get along and see eye to eye on what you both expect. Get a feel for how responsive the editor is. Is he or she willing to update you as often as you want?

Remember it's your book. You control it. You have the final say over whether to follow the advice from the editor.

Get a quote from the editor. If they aren't willing to give a project quote, then get a maximum and minimum amount that they will charge. Most of all, know what you are paying for.

Set benchmarks so that you can head off any potential problems that arise and have an early out plan if things just don't work out.

Consider Your Market

As you consider indie publishing a book, whether it is an e-book or physical, consider who you are trying to reach with the book. Even if you eventually expand the market to include additional segments of the population, you need to start with a definable market in order to get traction.

When I was getting ready to write my first historical novel, my first thought was that I wanted to reach readers of historical novels. That was a pretty broad market. It included things like steampunk, historical romance, westerns, WWII novels, world history novels, and on and on. It was also a market that told me my publisher at the time wouldn't want my novel, so I knew I would either have to find a new publisher or do it myself.

I tried to focus that broad historical fiction market even further. Since the novel was about the C&O Canal, I decided that my primary market was people who were interested in the canal and its history. This would be in large part people who visited the canal. The C&O Canal had six visitor centers along its 184-mile length at the time. It also ran through various towns. I realized that all of those places were within a couple hours of where I lived. I could visit those sites and get my book into stores along the route.

With this picture of my market, I was able to formulate a successful plan to reach them. In this case, it involved a lot of in-person sales. Other titles have led to me focusing on different areas or using forms of paid and non-paid advertising.

As my canal novel sold more copies and garnered positive reviews, I added additional audiences into my focus area. Some of this was determined by where I saw my books selling.

You can't simply depend on bookstores anymore to sell your book, and you definitely cannot depend on your publisher. You've got to think outside the box. Don't think about getting on the bestseller list. If you do that, you're going to have to sell primarily through stores that have their sales recorded by whichever list you want to appear on. If you're thinking outside the box, you won't be relying on those stores so even if you are selling at bestselling levels, it won't show. Let that be icing on the cake if it happens. What you want to do is reach your audience and make a profit doing it.

Strategy Tip: *While it is nice to have a book take off and rocket to the top of the charts, one of the advantages of indie publishing is that you can slowly grow your sales and turn your book into a perennial strong seller. It is like starting with a small snowball and rolling it down a hill. It will grow in both size and speed.*

Layout and Design

Whether you do e-books or physical books, you will need to lay out and design them. You can certainly hire someone to do this for you, but that will add to the bottom line you need to clear before you can start making a profit. Whichever way you choose, you should still be aware of some of the principles of layout and design.

You can find lots of programs to do layout with. Quark, InDesign, and Publisher are some of the popular programs. I have found, though, that for a typical one-column book (most novels), Word works fine.

Strategy Tip: *When I was developing the settings and other choices that worked for me, I looked at what mainstream publishers had done. They had been publishing far longer than me, so I knew they had learned what worked best. Unless I had a reason to do something differently than them, I used their books as my pattern.*

If you are using a book printer, he will provide the page guidelines. If you are using KDP (Kindle Direct Publishing, which is Amazon.com's self-publishing division), you can download templates that are already set.

Some basics are that I typically use Times New Roman 12 pt. type for my body font. I might get a little fancier with title and subhead fonts, but you want an easy-to-read font. Times New Roman, Garamond, and Georgia are popular fonts for the body.

I used to use 11 pt. type for my books, but then older readers started asking me about large-print editions. That was not a viable option for me, but bumping up the size of the font to 12 pt. has been a good compromise.

You also want to justify both sides of your text. This creates an attractive straight line formed from the text down both sides of the page. You can see that on the pages of this book.

The following images are screenshots of the formatting boxes you will need to complete to set up a book in Word. I will tell you the settings I use and have found work best, but your book is your project. You can start with my settings and see how changing them affects your project.

The first thing I set is the page size for the book. In Word, go to Page Layout > Size > More Paper Sizes. An image like the one on the next page should pop up.

On this page you will enter the size of the book, you are producing. These are the settings for the size book I typically publish. However, I decided to make this book slightly smaller, and I often do my longer novels as a 6 x 9-inch book.

You can play around with different sizes to see what best meets your needs. I chose to use the larger page size for some novels as a cost-saving measure. Print-on-demand (POD) books charge by the page no matter what the size is. So a 6 x 9 300-page book costs the same to print as a 5 x 8 300-page book.

This next image shows the margin settings for a book. You get there by clicking on the Margins tab on the same box where you set the page size.

The margins are important because you don't want the text running too close to the edge of a page where it might be cut off or crimped in the spine.

Page Setup   ?   ✕

Margins	Paper	Layout

Margins

Top: 0.35"   ▲▼   Bottom: 0.35"   ▲▼

Inside: 0.88"   ▲▼   Outside: 0.5"   ▲▼

Gutter: 0"   ▲▼   Gutter position: Left

Orientation

[A] Portrait   [A] Landscape

Pages

Multiple pages: Mirror margins   ▼

Preview

Apply to: This section   ▼

Set As Default   OK   Cancel

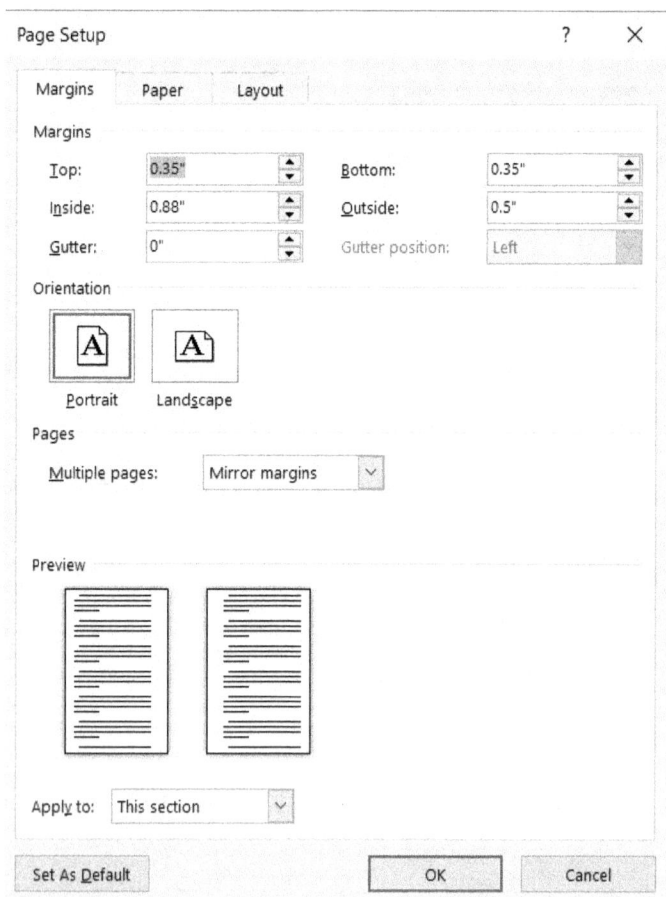

I initially tried KDP's templates for my books, but the result always appeared like the margins were too wide. So I began experimenting and landed on these settings. They will work for other size books as well. You will also want to make sure the page is oriented for portrait (taller than it is wide) unless you are doing something like a photography or coffee-table book. Most people expect a portrait-oriented book.

Now, choose Mirror margins. This allows the program to change automatically the inside and outside margins of your page depending on which side of the page will be bound. The margin settings then add a little more for the inside margin, so that the text won't get too close to where the pages are bound.

Next you want to set the headers and page numbering. Select Insert > Header > Edit Header. This will open a new tab called Design and put your cursor in the header. You want to make sure that Different First Page and Different Odd & Even Pages boxes are checked.

You then need to create a header for the first page, odd pages, and even pages of the document. You do this by creating the headers you want in the document. The first instance will be the template used for the rest of the document.

For page numbers, select Insert > Page Number. Then select the type of page number you want. You will also need to do this for the first page, odd pages, and even pages.

The document will use these as the template for each new section. Each chapter is a new section in my books. I mark it this way by going to Page Layout > Breaks > Section Breaks > Next Page.

Next, select Home > Paragraph, and you will see this page.

Paragraph ? ×

Indents and Spacing   Line and Page Breaks

General

Alignment: Centered

Outline level: Body Text   ☐ Collapsed by default

Indentation

Left: 0"   Special: By:
Right: 0"   (none)

☐ Mirror indents

Spacing

Before: 0 pt   Line spacing: At:
After: 0 pt   Multiple   1.1

☐ Don't add space between paragraphs of the same style

Preview

CRITICAL ACCLAIM FOR

Tabs...   Set As Default   OK   Cancel

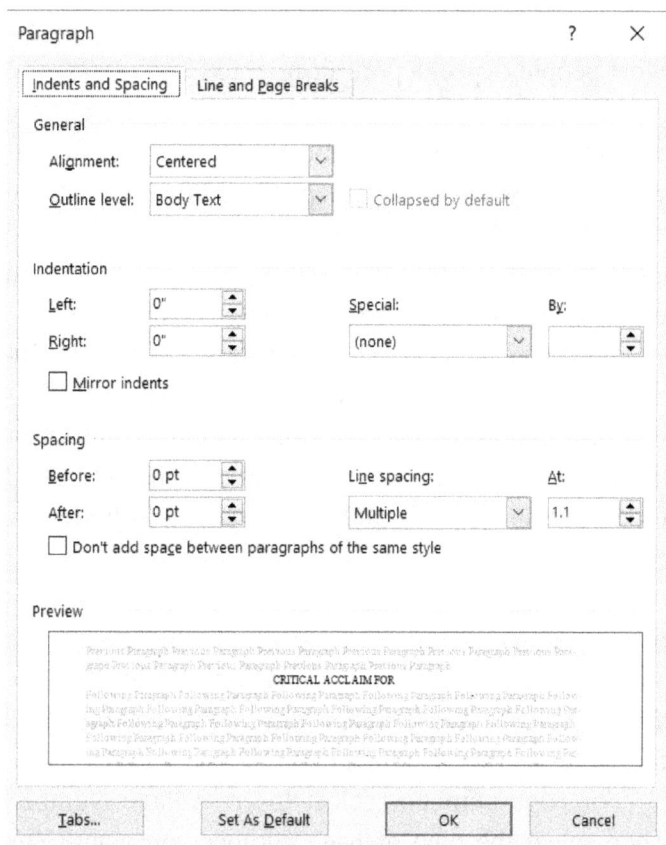

I used to make my books single spaced, but that final product can look crammed. Nowadays, I use the Multiple 1.1 or 1.08 line spacing. This opens up the text on the page and makes it easier to read.

Also, under the Line and Page Breaks tab, make sure Widow/Orphan Control and Keep with Next aren't checked. If they are, you might wind up with some odd-looking gaps at the bottom of some pages depending on how long your paragraphs are.

Strategy Tip: *Once you have successfully published a book, don't reinvent the wheel with the next one. Use the first book as your template for the next one. Settings you know work will be in place, and all you might need to do is change some title fonts and perhaps do a little format tweaking.*

Cover Design

Your book cover needs to catch the reader's eye, so you want it to look brilliant and professional.

I showed you earlier how using a graphic designer can improve your book.

If you want to try it yourself, you can use a program like Publisher to create a workable cover. E-books require .jpg images as the final product. For a physical book, you will need a .pdf as the final product. Publisher will save your files both ways.

You will need to consult the platform where you are publishing to find out how that platform wants the cover file prepared. Two of the leading platforms—Amazon and IngramSpark—both want cover files in a different way.

JAMES RADA JR.

In addition to the exterior dimensions of a book cover, you will also need to calculate the width of the spine. The platform will have instructions for how to calculate this measurement.

You can see how it is easier to hire an experienced designer to worry about it for you.

Choose a Printer

The first thing you need to consider is what you're looking for. There are printers, POD publishers, and vanity.

Vanity – This would be the worst way to go, but some people still choose it because it can sound good. You might pay up to three times more than getting the services another way. For all that money you pay, you only get a few copies of your book. Bookstores tend to know who these publishers are and not carry them. You are overpaying to be published.

POD – This is a very affordable printing option. You pay for what services you want and for how many copies you need. The price per copy is the same, no matter how many copies you buy. It is usually your best choice unless you are either printing color inside the book or printing a thousand or more copies at once.

Book Printer – You submit your project, and they print it. They can also provide some extras. Most printers have website with a way to request a quote.

Fill out the information and get the pricing back. Prices can vary, so get at least three quotes. Keep things the same so you can compare quotes between printers.

Also, look at local printers. If you can drive to the printer and pick up your books, you will save on shipping charges.

Once you have the quotes, you can see who has the low bid. Make sure they are offering you what you want. Ask to see a sample of the printer's work. Look at both the total cost and the unit costs. The total cost will tell you if you can afford it. The unit cost will give you an idea of what your retail cost will need to be to make a profit.

LONG-TERM GOALS

The thing to keep in mind as you go about trying to find freelance work is that you are trying to build a business and not simply get a single assignment. This doesn't mean you should turn down any one-off assignments, though. Just look for long-term projects and people who need work done frequently. These clients will be editors and department heads who like your writing. They will be your bread and butter.

These types of clients are important because it will save you time. If you need to query for every assignment, you use up a lot time. I write three newspaper columns, which require regular work. Plus, one of those newspaper editors contacted me to do a monthly series of articles about the Civil War year. Another editor calls me when she has events and other stories she needs covered.

Getting these types of clients can also create word of mouth as editors talk to each other. I got a call once from a regional magazine about writing some lifestyle articles. It turns out that the editor of the magazine had gotten my name from a newspaper editor I worked with.

Developing Relationships with Editors

I mentioned earlier the importance of developing a good relationship with an editor. So, why should you want to do this?

Once editors know your work and know you as a writer, you can become someone they can depend on, a go-to writer. Remember, chances are they work with a lot of writers and not all of them are as professional as you are going to be.

For you, this means that you'll get your stories accepted easier and faster with an editor who knows you. A borderline idea might be rejected if the editor doesn't know the writer, but if editors know you, they may be more willing to take a chance with the story.

Another nice thing is that once editors know you, they may get in touch with you to write articles for them. I've had that happen with several magazines. It's nice to get a guaranteed sale that I don't need to solicit. It saves you time trying to sell that idea, and for a writer who is trying to make a living, the more time you can put toward making money rather than marketing, the better.

To develop a good relationship with editors, you simply need to do two things: produce good work consistently and be easy to work with. That makes an editor's job easier and they will appreciate you for it.

1. **Reply quickly to any inquiries made by editors** – You would like them to do it for you, so do it for them. This includes being quick about proofing your own articles that are sent to you.

2. **Be willing to be edited** – Don't fight every change that the editor wants to make to your article. Most of the time, the changes will improve your work. Even if you don't think the change improves your work, unless it makes the article incorrect, you are probably better off not fighting it too much. Remember, the editor is paying for the article. If the change makes the editor happy, then he or she will be happy with you.

3. **Add extra information if you can** – Provide captions and photo credits for any photos you submit. If appropriate, add a sidebar.

4. **Add extra photos** – If you are submitting pictures with your article, supply more than is needed, so the editor has a good selection to choose from.

5. **Keep to the work length assigned for the story** – The word count is assigned for a reason. It is based on the space allocated for the story. If you write longer or shorter than the word count, then you will create extra work for the editor, which won't be appreciated.

6. **Produce quality work** – Write a good story that readers like and keeps them wanting more.

Become an Expert

Another way that you will come to be in demand is if you are seen as an expert in a subject. This recognition will happen with time and experience. As you consistently work with a magazine, your work may tend to fall into a niche. My niche is usually seen as history, but I've done multiple stories for one magazine that accidentally turned out to be health stories, so that magazine now considers me a health writer.

As you develop your expertise, editors will begin to recognize you as an expert in that field or at least someone who can write on that topic. That's when you become the magazine's go-to writer on the topic. It doesn't mean you can't pitch the magazine other ideas. You will just be known better for writing on a different topic.

When I first contacted the editor of *Allegany Magazine* about writing stories for him, he was very excited because he was a fan of my history column so he knew my work and was anxious for me to do local history for the magazine.

I know a man in Cumberland who became known for his historical knowledge of western Maryland. He collected historic postcards and pictures for years about western Maryland. Throughout the 1980s and 1990s, he published them in numerous books. He is considered the go-to man for local history in Cumberland, and he is the first person everyone thinks about when they need a photo, a judge, a speaker, etc.

The benefit of becoming an expert is that when the editor is looking to assign a story in your niche, you'll be the first person to come to mind. The bad news is that you won't be the first person to come to mind if it's not your niche.

Another aspect of becoming an expert includes becoming an expert writer. I've been writing professionally since 1988, and I still look for ways to improve and expand my skills. I still attend writers conferences and take classes on writing. Never stop learning.

Other Streams of Revenue

Once you have written a book or even become recognized as an expert in a particular area, you will want to consider how to earn income by creating other streams of revenue.

There are a variety of ways to do this. It is a matter of finding the ways that match your personality, and in some cases, your product.

Earning money from varied streams of income is also a form of diversification, and I am all for that. Publishing in different formats and different genres and building on that through other forms of income-generating content will help smooth out your income. If you are writing westerns and that market disappears, you are in trouble. However, if you write westerns and romances or even western romances, you can weather the storm. When COVID hit, my physical books sales dried up, but my e-book sales took off because people stuck at home wanted something to do. They could download an e-book and start reading right away and not have to wait for the mail to deliver a physical book.

Developing other streams of revenue will help you get maximum exposure and maximum income.

Giving a talk at a local historical society allowed me to earn a speaker's fee and sell my books afterward.

If You Published a Book

I consider this the easiest way to begin creating other streams of revenue. Most Americans (75 percent) have read at least one book in the past year, according to the Pew Research Center. So, if you've written a book, you have a chance to reach three out of four Americans unless you only publish in a single format.

Pew Research has also shown that 65 percent of people have read a physical book, 30 percent have read an e-book, and 23 percent have listened to an audiobook. To have a chance at attracting that 75 percent figure, you need to make sure you publish your book in multiple formats because some people read or listen to only one format.

While audiobooks can be expensive to produce, you should at least publish your book as a paperback and e-book. This will increase your reach, your sales, and your revenue.

Building on Books

Once you have a book published or a reputation as an expert, you can build on that. I give a lot of talks at libraries and historical societies. Some of these places will pay me a speaker's fee, but all of them allow me to sell my books after my talk.

Now, if your book or expertise isn't in history,

you will want to consider other venues. Children's book writers will talk at schools. I have a friend who writes mysteries, and she is doing a talk at a winery where people pay a fee that gets them a drink and a copy of her latest book. The goal for the winery is that hopefully people will buy more drinks or bottles of their wine. Meanwhile, the author gets the fee for each attendee.

You can also teach courses based on your book topic. I did this for years. I can't say that it sold more of my books, but I got paid well for teaching the courses. I wouldn't have been able to get those teaching jobs without having the credentials of being a published author.

Strategy Tip: *Community colleges are a great place to start looking for teaching opportunities. Many colleges have non-credit courses for the community on a variety of topics. Because these are non-credit courses, you shouldn't need a master's degree to teach them as you would a credit course.*

Other Ways to Generate Income

Here are some additional ways you can create additional income from your existing products. Different people will get different results from them, so experiment until you find which ones work best for you.

Also, it doesn't hurt to re-evaluate from time to time. As your audience grows, you may have a better results from poor-performing methods.

Affiliate marketing links – If your website gets a lot of traffic, consider adding affiliate links. These are codes that are added to a link from your website that will give you credit for directing that person to another website to purchase a product.

You can join an affiliate program for a product you like and want to sell on your website, or you can simply join Amazon's affiliate program. This is what I use currently.

I add the code that leads to Amazon page to all my book links. If a person clicks on the link and purchases the book, I get a little extra from Amazon. If they make any purchases from Amazon for a few days afterward, I will also get a small percentage of those sales.

Specific product links are generally what other companies use. If you promote a software program on your site and someone clicks the link to go to that website and then purchases the product, you will get a commission on that sale.

Sponsored content – If you have a platform on some place like YouTube or Instagram, or you have a podcast, you may be able to find a company to sponsor your content. Usually, you will need to mention or show the product and promote it, although not so much that it becomes annoying to your followers.

Online courses/workshops – If you have written about a particular topic that lends itself to instruction on how to accomplish something, you might consider creating an online course or workshop. There are a variety of ways this can be done. Some will require more effort from you to set up. I decided to try this out by teaching an online course through a writer's organization I belong to. I got a percentage of the enrollment fee and the group got a portion for setting things up, managing the platform, and advertising it. For my part, I just had to teach the class and advertise it. It was relatively easy, and it allowed me to evaluate how deep I want to go into the online teaching realm.

Subscriptions – If you can produce regular content, say an e-zine, you might want to consider having readers pay subscriptions that would allow them access to a website behind a paywall or receive content via e-mail.

Advertising – You can place ads on your website that will pay you when people click on the ad to go to the advertised product.

Merchandise – Perhaps, there is merchandise you can create to complement your books. You can sell this on your website. T-shirts are a popular item, but there are lots of other things that can be sold.

I like doing this, although I don't do it from my

website yet. I use the merchandise to increase the appeal of my booth at shows where I sell directly to the public.

I will also evaluate how that merchandise sells from time to time. If something stops selling, I will phase it out and introduce something new.

Donations/tips – If you don't want to feel like you are selling all the time, you might add a tip or donation button to your website or social media platform. I have seen this becoming more popular on YouTube with independent content creators.

Consulting/coaching – Of the mentioned ways to create additional streams of income coaching, consulting, and editing can generate the most income. However, it is not scalable, which means it has a limited potential based on the amount of time you have that can you can put toward helping someone else achieve their dreams and goals.

Earn Money from Books before Publication

Writing a book and earning royalties isn't the only way you can make money from your book and it's certainly not the fastest way. Even before your book hits the shelves, you can be making money from your research by creating articles related to your book topics. Not only will you create an additional revenue stream for yourself, you will help create interest in your book when it is released.

When you wrote your book, whether it was fiction or non-fiction, you most likely did research to make it authentic. That knowledge you now have can be turned into several different articles, each of which will earn you additional income, increase exposure of you as an expert on a subject that book explores, and increase exposure of your book.

By using your research to create articles to help market your book, you'll help increase your sales so that when those royalties come in, they will be larger than they otherwise might have been. The other way articles will help increase your sales is that they will increase your reputation as an author of topics in whatever field you write about.

For example, if you write a historical novel set during the Civil War, you can sell articles about the Civil War based on your research to regional and history magazines. Those readers will become familiar with your name and your writing style and be more likely to buy your books.

How Do You Do It?

The big question is how do you take a 100,000-word book and turn it into a 1,000-word article?

Serialize – The most obvious answer is if your book is fiction, you can serialize it. You don't see a lot of magazines serializing novels anymore, and the serialization rights are usually part of your book contract, so if you haven't sold the book yet, you might be giving something away that could be valuable.

If you do serialize your novel, you can turn each chapter of your book into an article. Just imagine the extra revenue that could mean for you. Even if you run the article for free, you will still benefit from consistent, regular, and large exposure for your book. You probably couldn't afford that much advertising.

A variation on this that has started gaining some popularity is serialization on the Internet, either through your own website or an e-zine. Horror writer Doug Clegg serialized his novel *Nightmare House* on the Internet, and by the time the serialization ended, Cemetery Dance Books had given him a five-figure advance.

Summarize – For non-fiction books, the most-obvious answer for creating articles from your book is to write articles based on one of the concepts in your book. It can be as easy as taking a chapter from the book, reworking it so it has a beginning and end, and selling it as a stand-alone article. For books that don't easily breakdown to one idea per chapter, you can summarize a concept or idea into an article. Jeff Guinn did this with an article he wrote about Bonnie and Clyde in Smithsonian Magazine that was based on his book *Go Down Together*. Readers interested in the article would also be interested in the book.

New ideas – This method requires more work, but it can be more rewarding. Not all of your research on a topic makes it into a book, but it can be used to write articles. The article will still be about a topic found in your book. It just won't be as directly connected to your book.   When doing this type of article, consider your research, not necessarily your book. What ideas did you have when you were reading up on different subjects? Chances are someone else could find it interesting, too.

Localize – Localizing your research is a technique that local news media teach for how to handle national topics. You find a local connection to a national topic. It requires additional research, but you already know the basics of the topic from your initial research. With a localized topic, you can market articles to every regional magazine in the country. There are two big advantages with this technique. 1) Even though your book may not be about the local area, it can create interest with local readers for your book by making a local connection. 2) It's easier to create interest when you're writing about something closer to the readers.

You Already Laid the Groundwork

The thing about using your book to develop articles is that it should be easier than coming up with a completely original idea. After all, you are familiar with the subject and enjoy it enough to have written a book around it. Because you are familiar with the subject, it should be easier for you develop the query letter and write the article.

Your article will probably be around 800 words, though magazine editors will give you the word count that they need.

Though your article shouldn't necessarily be about your book, you should make sure to reference it and/or your website in the article or author bio. This usually comes as an author blurb at the end of the article so that you can tie it back to your book or web site. John Kremer wrote in *1001 Ways to Market Your Book* that indie-publishing gurus, Tom and Marilyn Ross, sold articles based on their books, and "In each case, they insisted that the magazine include an end-note telling readers where they could order the book."

Within the blurb, ask the reader to visit your website. In an ad, that would be a call to action. This call to visit your website should be the only place in your article where you promote yourself.

Don't Forget the Internet

Don't overlook websites as a location to publish your articles. If you can generate visitors to your website, and it can make a great place to serialize your novel.

On the Internet, your author blurb will become an active link to take the reader right to your website. You can also write articles as free content for other websites to attract readers to your website where you can hopefully entice them to buy your book and turn it into a bestseller.

In today's marketplace where catching a reader's attention can take some creative marketing, using your book to create articles will bring readers interested in your topic right to your doorstep. It will build your credibility in your field and increase your contacts with editors who might be willing to review or promote your books in other ways. Besides, how often do you get paid to market yourself and your books? Don't miss out on this chance.

THE BUSINESS SIDE OF WRITING

If you are going to work diligently at freelance writing and make money from it, you need to approach it as a business. For one thing, you will be expected to pay taxes on your writing income, so you need to track income and expenditures.

If you are just dipping yourself into the freelancing world, you may consider your work a hobby. The major difference between a hobby and a business from a tax perspective is that you can take a business loss during a bad year. With a hobby, you can only deduct up to the amount of money you earned.

Treating your freelance work as a business and acting in a professional manner also gives your client a greater comfort level in dealing with you.

So, let's look at what you need to be doing to get your business up and running.

Name

Do you need a business name? It depends on what type of writing you are doing. If you are doing magazine and newspaper writing only, you probably don't need a business name. If you are doing editing, it is a gray area where you can go either way. If you are doing e-publishing, then you want a publishing name.

As a book author, you will get asked, "Who publishes you?" It's not a question I think I would ask an author, but it is something that I get asked a lot. I will either say, "I am indie published" or "AIM Publishing," which is my business name. A business name will also help if you are trying to set up wholesale accounts. Many companies would rather deal with a business when setting wholesale accounts.

Some people recommend a genre-specific name for your company because it tends to stand out among generic names. That is true, but I don't think the publishing name needs to stand out. It simply needs to imply you aren't a one-person operation.

The problem with a genre-specific name is what if you want to expand into other genres? I chose an umbrella name with plans for different imprints. Honestly, if I had it to do over again, I probably would have just published everything under my umbrella name, but I had already published under "Legacy Publishing" when I decided to do a horror novel. I believed

Legacy Publishing would not have worked since it implied more historical imagery than horror. It wouldn't have been a major problem, but at the time, I was considering every detail as to how I presented the book. So I had to create a new imprint.

Once you have a name in mind, do a web search and see if anyone else is using it. While this doesn't mean you can't use the name (unless it's been trade-marked), you might be setting yourself up for problems down the line. I ran into this problem with one of the companies that buys for the national parks. I had trouble getting paid for a while because my invoices kept getting confused with another Legacy Publishing they worked with. Luckily, I had established AIM Publishing Group by then, so I had them invoice that company.

Business Setup

You will want to do some other items to help your business run.

Banking – Set up a checking account so you can pay company bills. The cheapest way to do this is set up business checking under your name with DBA. DBA means "doing business as."

With this designation, you will be able to deposit checks made out to either you or the business. An account for your business also helps keep your funds separate to make bookkeeping easier.

Type of business – A sole proprietorship will suit most people, though some people may form an LLC, corporation, or partnership. A sole proprietorship just requires you to fill out a Schedule C and pay quarterly taxes. If you begin to take on employees, you may want to create some legal separation between you and your business and the other forms begin to do that.

Business address – You're most likely going to be running your business out of your home. In some places, local zoning may frown on this, but if you're not obvious (bringing in a lot of people), then work from home. You may want to consider a post office box, though. I tried it that way and didn't like it. It means having to make regular trips to the post office to collect mail.

Phone – Do you want to receive calls on your personal phone? If you do use your phone for work, you can deduct a portion of the costs. If you get a separate line for business, it's an additional expense. Just about every author I know uses their own phone.

E-mail and website – When you create your website (www.YOURNAME.com), it will probably come with the ability to create e-mail addresses, using your site name. You can even set these addresses up to forward to your regular e-mail if you want. You can also keep them with your website to separate your personal and business e-mails.

Storage – You're going to need physical storage space. It needs to be a dry area. If you go with a book printer, you will need a lot of space for 1,000 books or more. One of the advantages of POD is that I can order books as I need them, and they print and ship quicker than a book printer can do the job. I generally keep a few dozen copies of each of my books on hand. Since I have twenty-nine titles out, that is around 1,000 books I have to find a place to store.

Sales tax license – You will want to register for a sales tax license. The disadvantage is that you will have to file a short quarterly or semi-annual tax form that shows how much you made in taxable sales and then submit the sales tax for it. The advantage is that with a license, you won't have to pay tax on the books you have printed for sale. Also, if you do a lot of events each year like I do, you won't have to apply for a temporary license for each event. I probably save at least $1000 a year doing this. Starting out, you won't need it right away because the volume of books you are selling probably won't justify it, but it is something you will eventually want to get.

Tax ID number – If you are operating as a sole proprietorship, you can use your Social Security Number as your tax identification number. If you don't feel comfortable using your Social Security Number or you have another form of business structure, you can apply for an Employee Identification

Number from the IRS. It can be done online or using Publications 1635.

Business license – Whether you need a business license to operate out of your home will vary from jurisdiction to jurisdiction. Check with your town or county for the requirements in your area.

Terms and Conditions

You need to have terms and conditions that you can send to potential vendors. Even if you never send it to a vendor (I haven't in years), having it written down allows you to treat vendors in the same way and offer the same discounts.

Your terms and conditions need to outline what constitutes an acceptable return, pricing, volume discounts, payment terms, shipping, and ordering. For articles and other works, you will want to outline when you expect payment and the pricing you basing quote on. Even if you never present these to your customers, it gives you a baseline to work from.

You will run into vendors from time to time who have their own terms and conditions. They may expect a different discount or pay invoices later. I write for magazines that pay on publication and others that pay on acceptance of my story. I work with some clients who pay when I complete the work and others who want to be invoiced. It is up to you whether you will accept their terms or forego their business.

Distribution vs. Wholesale

If you are publishing a book, you will be dealing with wholesalers and distributors, so you need to understand the difference.

Distributors – Distributors sell books on consignment supported by a sales force. Typically, they take 35 percent of the retail price.

Wholesalers – Wholesalers are widely available and widely used. They will stock your book and send it to retailers and distributors that request it. Typically, wholesalers take 55 percent of the retail price.

Direct to stores – Sell direct to stores if you can. You cut out the middle man and keep more of the cover price. Typically, they want a 40 percent discount off the cover price or 20 percent if they are selling your book on consignment.

While you can make more money selling direct to stores, it will take more time. You need to contact them occasionally, stop in and say "hi," check on inventory, offer to sign books, etc. However, customer service can pay off with larger orders from these stores.

Now, if you go the publishing route I've talked about with KDP (Amazon) and Ingram, not only are they acting as your book printer, they will act as your wholesaler and distributor. I am all for keeping things simple.

If you use a book printer, you will need to contact Ingram and Baker & Taylor and establish your own accounts with them. They will send you purchase orders telling you how many copies of each title to send to various warehouses. You are then responsible for the shipping and billing. It is more complicated and less profitable.

Taxes

A business needs to show a profit three out of five years. This means you have more deductions you make.

Besides, filing your annual tax form, which can be done on Schedule C if you are you filing as an individual proprietorship. You will also need to file quarterly tax forms. This is you paying what would usually be deducted from your paycheck if you were an employee.

As your business grows, you can become a corporation, which will require different forms.

Though you can have someone do your taxes for you, I've come to prefer doing them myself. It's a bit more time-consuming, but no one's going to dig for deductions better than you. I use TaxCut, which allows me to make changes easily and see how they affect everything else.

Running your freelancing as a business allows you to write off part of your home expenses based on the percentage of your home that you use as an office and your car expenses as well. Those are nice deductions to have, particularly since you have to pay both sides of your FICA taxes (Social Security and Medicare taxes).

At the beginning of the year, you can expect to receive 1099s from clients for whom you performed a lot of work (over $600). These forms will simply say how much they paid you and reported to the IRS. You won't see taxes deducted, which means you need to set money aside for quarterly taxes.

By the same token, if you paid outside help more than $600 in a calendar year, you will most likely need to file a 1099 for them. The advantage would be that if you had an assistant, you would have to be dealing with payroll taxes. It is much simpler just to pay directly to the help and let them deal with it.

Rate Setting

With magazines and newspapers, you won't have much say over your rate. You basically accept what they are willing to pay or not. The real difference is some of the extras. Does the magazine pay mileage? Do you get paid extra for photos? How long is the piece? You need to consider these things and decide if your total income from the article is worth it. When I wrote an article about the Tuskegee Airmen years ago, I thought I'd get $100 for the article, but I also provided historic photos. I didn't ask for pay since I didn't take the pictures. I just found them and made sure the magazine could publish them. I got paid for the pictures anyway, an additional $125.

With other projects, there is room for negotiation. However, you need to make the first move and set the rates that you feel your project is worth.

You can set an hourly rate for everything or an hourly rate for the type of work. This can become of complicated mix of calculations as you consider expenses, time, materials, and needed profit.

Strategy Tip: *If a client wants an hourly rate, I have found it much easier to rely on work that has been done by organizations. If you belong to a writing organization, it will often have a list of rates among its members for different types of work. The prices will often include a range charged for that particular service. I tend to stay near lower middle of the range. The higher end are rates charged by highly experienced writers (which I am) living in a high cost-of-living location (which I don't).*

While it might be easier to quote an hourly rate, that usually doesn't work for me. I recently quoted a project that the client estimated would take 25 hours.

I did it in 15. I was expecting one price, but I'll get paid another because the client wanted to be billed hourly.

If you are a fast writer, quoting a project cost will be the best way to go. The client knows exactly what the bill will be and you maximize your hourly rate.

I reserve charging an hourly rate as much as possible for when I am working in a new area that might have a learning curve.

Finally, don't count on getting paid until you see the money in the bank. Even with reliable clients, it may take months until you get paid. However, if you receive no payment after you should have and you have notified the client repeatedly, you will have to decide whether you want to take the client to court or write it off. Mostly likely, it will be cheaper just to write off the expense and never work with that client again.

Contracts

You will want to have a contract between you and the client for writing projects. If the client doesn't have one, then you will need to create one.

They don't need to be complicated. They do need to lay out what is expected from each party, what the final deliverable to the client will be, the costs, and the deadline for completion. You might also include an agreement about how overruns will be handled if you think it will be an issue. You can include mention of a late fee for overdue accounts, but I have found that companies that pay late will probably ignore the late fees, too.

Since most of your work will be via e-mail, you can either mail the contracts for signatures or set up an account with an e-sign program.

If the client is reluctant to sign a contract, explain that it protects both of you. Be willing to talk about any issue that they have a problem with.

However, if the client won't sign a contract, my advice is to not take the job. You are asking for trouble. The client is likely someone who will nitpick issues and maybe not even pay. Don't give yourself that headache.

As I mentioned earlier, trying to get a deadbeat client to pay is often more trouble than it is worth. I am willing to take the first step, which is to make calls and send letters to the company.

If this fails, then you have to make the decision on whether to litigate. This creates an additional expense for you, and even if you win, the client can still find ways to stonewall you.

In the end, it is probably easier, cheaper, and less stressful simply to take the tax write-off. Then you can also notify any professional organizations that the company is part of the company's unethical practice. This will help other writers avoid the problem with a non-paying client.

Time Management

As you start your freelance career, particularly when you are full time, you need to be aware of a few cautions because they can sneak up on you and cause problems.

You have a lot of freedom as a freelance writer and a lot of control over where your career will go.

Set your priorities before you even start freelancing. The reason for this is that it is easy to get lost in your work, particularly when you start coming up against deadlines.

When you work for someone else, you get paid for your time on the job and not directly for how much work you do. As an employee, you get paid for those side conversations you have with fellow workers or when you take a bathroom break. As a freelancer, you get paid when you complete a project to your client's satisfaction.

Don't ignore the fact that you have a life outside of work. You may be working at home, but that doesn't mean your work and home life should be one and the same. Make time for your family and friends. Make time yourself.

Create a personal schedule. The flexibility of freelancing is a wonderful plus to the work, but if you take it too far, the lack of structure can keep you from

getting things done because you would rather be doing something else. For instance, I got into a groove
while writing this book and wanted to work on it a lot
more than I really had time for. I had other projects
on deadline that needed to be written or edited. I had
to set limits on how long I would work on this book
each day in order to get everything done that needed
to be completed.

If you're more creative in the morning, you might
want to do the bulk of your writing in the morning. If
you like to stay up late at night, you can include the
late hours as part of your workday. If you have children, set your work hours to when they are asleep and
in school. I like to take a nap mid-afternoon when my
energy is at a low. Your job is not nine to five. You
don't have to treat is like it is.

The most effective thing I do to manage my
time is to write out a to-do list each day. I write
what I want to achieve for the day and then set out
to make that happen. Checking things off the list is
great positive reinforcement, and when I complete
the list, I don't feel guilty about stopping my work
for the day.

A list helps you develop discipline, which is a
necessary part of freelancing. If you don't have it,
you will fail because you will find other things to do
rather than a project you aren't really interested in.
Worse, you might keep putting that project off and
miss your deadline. That means you won't get paid.

Besides the daily list of things I need to do, for larger projects, I will set mini-deadlines in order to keep the project on track and not have to put an inordinate amount of time in on it at the end.

Time Off

There will be times when you need to not work either by necessity (illness) or by plan (vacation). While you won't get paid for either, it doesn't mean you shouldn't take the time off.

I try to schedule my vacations for the time of year when I have the least amount of work going on. For me, that tends to be the first quarter of the year. When my kids were younger, this was a time when it was nearly impossible to get away. Now, that they are out of school and don't even have to go with my wife and me on vacation, it is easier to take that time off. I have even been known to use a writer's conference or an event where I am staying overnight as a mini-vacation. When I get back to my hotel room at the end of the day, I might go sightseeing, swimming in the pool, or call it a day and go to sleep early. All of those things help recharge my body's energy reserves.

Because I know I will be taking a vacation, I first look at any projects that will come due during the time I am off. If I can make arrangements to change the due date, I will. If I can't, then I create my own deadline to have the project completed before my vacation. This may increase my workload in the week or two leading up to vacation, but sometimes it is necessary.

Now, me being me, I will often do a little work while on vacation. Usually this amounts to me working on a new story I am excited to write. Because I am excited about the project and in a different location, it feels more like fun than work to me. I recently wrote a short story for an anthology while I was relaxing all day at a beach in Galveston. I wrote it in chunks between napping, watching the waves, talking to my wife, and walking on the beach.

While I do put an out-of-office auto-reply on my e-mail when on vacation, I still check it, although I may not rush to reply. I may even answer my phone for a work call if I am not doing anything at the time.

Just don't ignore taking vacation time. Burnout from too much work can cause you to be off work for a lot longer than your vacation.

Burnout

It is easier to hold burnout at bay than it is to recover from it. To avoid burnout, you need to include exercise in your daily routine and work to get a good night's sleep each night. Sometimes, a change of scenery might be all I need. I will take my laptop and work into the sunroom at my house or go the nearby Panera restaurant and write there while eating a salad.

I can usually feel burnout creeping up on me. I feel a sense of dread about work or an unusual tiredness. If I already have a vacation planned that isn't too far off, I will keep working. If I don't have some time off planned soon, then I will do my best to free up an entire day where I don't have to work. I may do something fun, or in some cases, I have been known to lie around all day and sleep a lot. I try to listen to what my body is telling me.

Definitely don't ignore your health. Besides making sense in a broad sense for how it will improve your quality of life, it will help you in your work. Exercise releases endorphins that improve your mood. I also find they improve my creativity. When I take a walk, it frees my mind, and I often find ideas for stories popping into my mind. I will pull out my phone and start recording my thoughts to refer to later.

Make sure to get a good night's sleep and try to maintain a normal workday. These things will help you avoid burnout and extend your career as a freelancer.

Take at least one day off from work a week. This is particularly difficult for me. A lot of events I do are on the weekends. This means I should take a day off during the week, but I feel guilty doing it. As a compromise, I will work a couple half-days during the week. The idea is that it frees my mind from work and allows my creative batteries to recharge.

Outside Help

One way to avoid burnout is to hire outside help to take certain tasks off your plate. This can be hard to do when you are starting out because of the cost. It is also the time you are least likely to need outside help because you have more time to format your books or manage your social media.

I'm at the point in my career where I measure whether I can make more doing something else other than a task I don't like or I'm not good at.

Currently, I use outside editors and cover designers for my books. It's an easy decision for me. Although I know I can do both tasks myself, not only do I know their work will be better, it would probably take me longer to do it. It is more cost-effective for me to pay them, get a great product, and save myself time when I could be doing something that earns me more money.

Take a look at two versions of the same book cover on the next page. I did the one on the left for an e-book. When I decided I wanted to produce a physical book, I hired a cover designer. I liked my general design, but I asked her if she could make it look better. She produced the version on the right. I think it's better. My designers get even more creative when I give them more freedom.

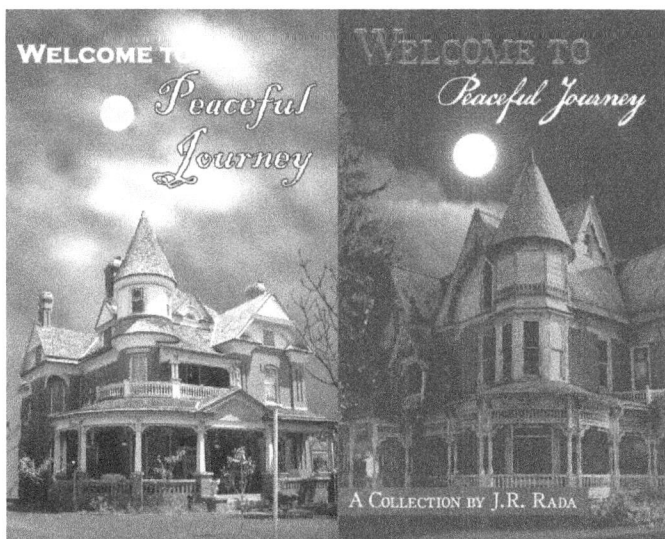

There are certainly other jobs I would prefer to have someone else do for me, such as managing my account books and social media. I haven't made that jump, though, for a couple reasons. First, by managing my own finances, I know where my money is going and if I'm overspending in an area. I know how much I need to earn to make my expenses. Second, you hear stories of shady accountants who cheated their clients. When you start looking for an accountant and asking around, you will probably hear stories that will worry you. Keep them in mind.

Research is another area I wouldn't mind having help with. However, when I do my own research, I often go off on tangents that lead to new ideas or deeper information about my topic. If I had a research assistant, he or she would stick to the topic I asked them to research and I might miss these additional ideas.

Finally, the act of hiring and managing outside help creates additional work for me and headaches as far as determining what I need from that help. I need to be sure the benefits of that help outweigh those new burdens.

YOUR PLATFORM

Have you ever wondered why a celebrity who can't write and might have trouble reading gets a big book contract? It's because they have an author platform.

You often hear people talk about a person's platform. Platform is how you reach an audience and how many people you reach doing it. It includes social media, but not just that. It can be blogs, podcasts, articles, professional communities, etc. I do dozens of shows and talks each year, and that is part of my platform, which probably adds up to at least a quarter million people. It is about your reach on those platforms. How many people are you reaching through your combined social media efforts? A good rough estimate of your reach is to add your following on various social media accounts and your e-mail lists. The greater your reach, the better, although you want to be giving your followers a reason to look at your accounts.

Having a large platform is why celebrities get book deals for lousy books. They can get their book known to lots of people and convince them to buy it. For publishers, this means they can estimate a minimum number of sales and know that it will be profitable even if the book is only good for a doorstop.

Mainstream publishers are also watching indie books, looking for ones to publish. If you are looking for a mainstream publishing deal, you will be more likely to get one if you can show you have a large platform and/or lots of book sales. However, I discovered, as many other indie authors have, that if you have a large platform and a lot of book sales, you don't need a mainstream publisher unless they bring some additional benefits for you to the table.

"Platform" differs from "Author Brand." Brand is the impression people get from your platform. It is why authors like myself use a pen name. For me, I use my name for history and historical fiction, but my fantasy, YA, and horror has a very different audience with different expectations, so I use J.R. Rada.

Platform is essential no matter whether you want one book or many, indie or traditional.

Even if your magnum opus isn't published yet, start building your platform now because it takes time.

Now, you can be published without a platform or much of one, but it makes it harder for that book to get traction. You will also need to focus your marketing more on book reviews and advertising.

You should start building your platform before

your book launches. This way, you will have something to work with when it does launch. It will also put you steps ahead of other authors who don't think about marketing until their book is published.

The best way to grow your platform is to make it fun for you to do. Incorporate the sites that work for you and that you enjoy using. I used to run a couple blogs, but they became a chore for me to do. I was also seeing little impact, so I stopped doing them. It took what had become a weight off my shoulders.

The thing you want is a way to consistently reach the audience and to do it in a way that's in your control. For instance, you can link your magazine articles as posts on your social media. This will hopefully get more eyes on the article than the magazine's average article and show the editor you have a social following that can help the magazine.

A Website

I recommend using your author name for your website (www.YOURNAME.com). This works whether you are freelance writing articles or indie publishing books. I tried a website once that was my company name, but people will be searching for you not your company.

The home page for jamesrada.com. It offers the latest news, my upcoming appearances, and an e-mail list sign-up. The picture at the top rotates through a series of historic images. Other pages on the site list my books, an about me page, a page for my pen name (I will eventually create another website for that), and a contact page.

Your website will be your central hub for your social media activity. You want to direct everyone to your website for more information about you.

Create an e-mail signature that includes your website. Add your website to your social media account profiles. Add it your business cards, show displays, and books. When you are interviewed, mention your website.

Send people to your website, and then make sure you update it regularly. Talk about your projects, where you will be signing books, new releases, media appearances, etc.

E-mail List

One thing I wish I had done early in my indie career was start building my e-mail list. This should be central to your platform because you control it. By collecting e-mail addresses from your readers, you won't lose access to them if your social media platform should decide to ban you. For instance, how would you contact all your followers on Facebook if your account got hacked or you got banned? Even if banning is a remote possibility, when you post something on Facebook, only a small portion of your followers see it on their news feeds. This is because Facebook changed their algorithms to encourage people to pay to boost their posts. If you send something to your e-mail list, everyone on the list gets it.

As you build your e-mail list, you should keep regular contact with your fans. I'm busy, but I manage two newsletters a month to different genre groups.

Your newsletter can be simple. My newsletters are usually a picture, an article (or story or preview) and a couple ads for other author books (I'll talk about newsletter swaps later). While you can ask them to buy your book, you shouldn't always write a sales pitch. Give your followers value added, so they will look forward to seeing your newsletter and open it and read it. If you are always trying to sell, sell, sell, your followers will start to delete your newsletters without reading them.

Along this same line, you may also want to have a reader magnet as an immediate reward for people who sign up for your mailing list. This might be a short story, deleted scenes, or even a free book. The idea is that it is an electronic freebie that can be sent at no cost to you to your mailing list members.

You will want to sign up for a service like Mailchimp or Mailerlite to help you manage your e-mail list. These services have a free version until you build your list to a certain size. The e-mail service also has templates for designing easy newsletters. They allow you to create different grouping of the e-mail addresses your collect to create targeted mailings, and they will send your newsletters out and measure the results.

They also have a feature for automating your contacts. What this does is when someone signs up for my newsletter, it connects to the e-mail service that sends out a series of e-mails at certain intervals. These automations welcome the new follower and send my reader magnets spaced out over a few weeks. When the automation sequence completes, the e-mail address is added to my list.

As you are building your platform, give the reader value. It can be direct: sign up for my mailing list and get X. Or indirect, like writing useful info on a blog and pitching your new books or having ads on your page.

Don't abuse the list – if you constantly pitch your services or your book, readers will tune out and then leave your list.

Think about it as paying it forward. Build some karma and relationships. I was watching a training video the other day. I forget what the woman was talking about, but she noted, "If a person likes you, they are more likely to read your books." Think about it in terms of your favorite authors. They release a new book. How likely are you to buy it without knowing anything other than who wrote it versus if the author was unknown? Don't look at platform building as marketing but as building relationships.

Part of the karma and relationship building effort is what I call the ripple effect. One of the reasons I like to sell at festivals is that I often meet people who ask me about speaking to their group. I also see, and I still can't understand why, spikes in my online sales. One reason I use a Buy 2, Get 1 Free deal is that not only does it encourages sales, but I know from speaking with the buyers, they often decide to buy a book for someone else. This gives me another potential reader to hook in.

Strategy Tip: *Add an embedded e-mail list sign-up form to your website. Since you are directing readers to your website as your central hub, it only makes sense to offer them a way to keep up to date with what is happening with you by signing up for your e-mail list.*

E-mail newsletters work best for book authors. It doesn't matter whether you are traditionally published or indie published. A newsletter gives you a way to communicate directly with your readers.

If you are a business writer, you can also make a newsletter work for you. I have seen professional business writers who have a mailing list of clients and potential clients. They will send them newsletter that contain useful information to someone who uses outside business writers. The clients can use the information, and the writer keeps his name in front of potential clients.

I can't say I have seen a feature or newspaper

writer create a newsletter. The goal of such a newsletter would be to direct readers to the writer's articles, but any increase in sales would not be directly attributable to the writer.

Reader Magnets, Giveaways, & Swaps

As I mentioned earlier, one way to encourage readers to sign up for your newsletter is to offer reader magnets, giveaways, and swaps.

Reader magnets are freebies you offer people who sign up for your newsletters. They provide you with their e-mail contact, and you send them a reader magnet. I send a few free novels from my back list. The magnet costs you nothing, but it is of value to your readers.

Besides the organic growth to your list, you can do newsletter swaps and giveaways. Newsletter swaps are when another author agrees to promote your book with a link to their e-mail list, and you do the same for the author. I usually send them to my reader magnet. This means I get lots of new sign-ups for my newsletter. If you are interested in trying this, check out Story Origin. The site has lots of features, but the one I like is that it facilitates newsletter swaps, making it easy.

Giveaways are when you offer a prize for people who enter your giveaway. You can find services that help with this, such as King Sumo. These sites help you put together your giveaway with some different options. Then you just need to list the giveaway on different giveaway sites. I have done this, and you will get a large surge in sign-ups for your newsletter, but after the giveaway, a lot of these people will drop off your list. The last time I did a giveaway, I think my mailing list showed a final increase of around 400 new subscribers.

I have to admit that I like seeing my list grow because I know when I have a new book launch and talk about it in a newsletter, it will have an impact on sales.

Strategy Tip: *If you want to increase the number of people who stay on your e-mail list, tailor your giveaways to something that ties in with reading or you. You will get more sign-ups for a gift card, but more people will stay if you are offering something like a library of books in a similar genre to yours.*

Social Media

Social media is almost a necessary evil, but you need to be careful. Surfing the sites can be a time suck, and if you say the wrong thing on them, you might get a lot of negative feedback.

Facebook, Twitter, and Instagram are the most-popular sites to use right now. There are other sites, such as forums that might specifically target your audience. Of the three, I only use Facebook. In my opinion, Twitter is far too negative. I have an account, but I can't remember the last time I posted anything. Instagram is just something I never got into, but my impression is that is image oriented.

Remember, I said your social media needs to be something you enjoy. If Twitter and Instagram are fun for you, go ahead and use them. They will help build your platform.

If you are using Facebook, you will want to create an author page, particularly if you are writing under a pen name. This will allow you to keep your personal stuff off the feed unless it is something you want to share with your readers. Also, when you start running Facebook ads, they will reference your author page.

Since social media is a time suck, I try to make one post a day and scroll through other posts when I am eating lunch or watching television. This consistency gives my posts the best chance of reaching someone since your posts don't show up in the newsfeeds of all your followers. Facebook does this to encourage users to pay to boost their posts so that more people see it. However, if you post daily, it is likely that all your followers will at least see one of your posts. This will help keep you in their minds when they think about looking for their next book to read.

If you are an article writer, you can post that you are looking for certain people to interview or direct message businesspeople you want to interview. You can post links to published articles you have out.

It's about keeping your name out there and communicating with readers.

Non-Social Media Network

Your platform can also include non-digital reach. Professional speakers have a large non-digital reach because of all the attendees to their talks. You will start to see this if you do talks as part of your marketing strategy.

You will network with other professionals you meet at events or through writers groups and organizations like Pennwriters.

Networking was not my thing at first, but because I saw a lot of success selling my books at events, I eventually got used to speaking with people, so I started doing talks and classes. Networking has been successful for me. Here are some of the benefits I have found:

- Authors I have met at shows have given me tips on improving my sales at shows.
- Authors I have met have told me about other shows I didn't know about.
- I have gotten interview and speaking requests

from people I met at shows.

- I have met aspiring authors who I have invited to the writers group I attend.

- I have met authors and shared a booth space to minimize costs at expensive shows.

- I have turned some customers into regular buyers who visit my booth every year to talk and buy my new book.

- I get direct feedback on my books from readers.

- And, of course, it is financially profitable.

Don't expect quick results. Your platform is built day by day, bit by bit.

As you do this, experiment. I am willing to try new shows and techniques. I keep what works and replace what doesn't.

Watch your time. You can find yourself sucked into managing your platform. Set a time limit that works for you and time yourself so you don't move into using social media to waste time.

Think of yourself as a spider. The larger the web you can build, the more likely you are to catch a fly. You can also catch more flies and bigger flies. And since you're a writer, you don't have to eat the flies!

Marketing

Marketing is critical to your success as a magazine writer or author, whether indie or mainstream. Mainstream publishers may do some marketing, but they are going to expect you to get out and do a lot. After all, it is your book.

Even if you don't want to write a book, you will need to market yourself in order to attract new clients or sell an article.

Getting Book Reviews

Once your book is ready for publication, set the publication date. You will use this date as you set your pre-orders and promotions. Most mainstream publishers like to make a push in spring (April, May), fall (September, October) and summer (June, July). Think about publishing outside these times to avoid heavy competition for your book. January through March are good months for small presses to publish. You also want to plan it ahead in time for reviewers to have a chance to preview. This could be as much as 3 to 4 months.

Knowing these time frames, you don't have to wait until your book is ready to go to press before planning some of these things. However, a reviewer is going to want a print-ready copy. For this reason, I don't rely on reviews with that kind of long lead time. I don't want to have a book ready to go, and then have it sit around for months waiting for a possible review. I look for people who will review my books once they are out.

Look for targeted websites for your genre or book blogs that review your type of books. Then see what their submission policy is. Don't forget radio shows, podcasts, and local television. They like to have guests on. Some authors don't feel they get a good return from doing these things, but I had a local bookstore owner tell me once that he always knew when I had been on a local radio program because he saw a surge in my book sales.

I use a lot of these review blurbs in the front matter of my books for a "Critics are praising…" page.

If you have any contacts with authors in your genre, you might ask them for a blurb you can use on your cover. Even if you don't know any, contact some of your favorite authors in your genre and see if they would be willing to give you a blurb.

Strategy Tip: *Nowadays, newsrooms operate with minimal staff. If you want a good chance of having a local or regional newspaper run a wonderful story about your book, write your own press release about your book. Focus on why someone will want to read it and not simply on the fact that it is being released. Include quotes from you, as if you were interviewed for the article. Include where it can be purchased and if you have events coming up in that newspaper's circulation area. Most importantly, include lines in the article that would read well as a cover or review blurb. E-mail the review, an author head shot, and picture of the book cover to whoever handles book reviews or features at the newspaper. Because the newspapers have a lot of space to fill with only so much time to generate copy, they will often run your press release verbatim. When that happens, you can quote your own press release in review blurbs and credit the newspaper.*

Non-Book Marketing

As I wrote earlier, your primary ways to get new article business is queries and approaching clients with a writer package highlighting what you can do.

For editing projects, you might peruse the job boards of any writing groups you belong to. Often, an author seeking an editor will post on those board.

For magazines, commit to sending out queries. Aim for one a week. When you get a no, turn the article around to another magazine.

For business/scientific, start networking in person, by mail, and with follow-up calls.

Do Internet marketing. Post on pertinent blogs, e-mail clients, social media, etc.

When you get an article published, try your best to get your website listed. Then the article can perform an extra service as an advertisement for you.

If you run across an ad, you might be able to do better, do a rewrite and send it to the client.

Offline Marketing

You should also be considering offline marketing as well as online marketing in your plans. As I write this, I have to leave for a talk at the local Rotary Club in an hour. I'll give a short talk about the topic of one my books and sell some books afterward. I will make a couple hundred dollars and get a free meal.

Civic groups are always looking for speakers. Start by contacting your local one, since there is a local connection. Make sure to focus your talk on something interesting to them. In other words, don't talk a lot about yourself. Talk about your topic.

Other possible places you might find speaking opportunities are libraries, historical societies (if you write history), book clubs, and schools.

Schools can be tough to get into. If you want to try, start with the PTA, librarian, or English teachers. If you get them behind you, they can help shepherd you through the process.

Strategy Tip: *To be more appealing as a speaker, I never ask for a speaker's fee, although some organizations will pay me. Instead, I ask to be allowed to sell my books after my talk.*

A popular form of offline marketing is book signings at bookstores. Honestly, I have had mixed results with this. It can be hit or miss. I am most successful at stores where my books already sell well.

Also, as an indie author, don't expect to get into Barnes & Noble. While they like to have local authors in, they can't carry your book if it is print on demand, and they can't bring in an author whose books they can't carry. It's a corporate policy and can be frustrating for the local managers. My experience, though, is that the sales I got through Barnes & Noble when I was using a book printer didn't offset the advantages of going print on demand.

My favorite type of offline marketing is craft festivals and book festivals. I lean more toward the craft festivals because I am usually one of only a few authors at the event, so I have less direct competition. I can do well at book festivals, but I am competing against dozens of authors. People, even avid readers, will only buy so many books at once. A craft show increases the odds that they are purchasing mine.

You will need to invest in the basics for a show. This includes a canopy, folding table, and chair. You will also want to add things like signage, table coverings, and display racks at some point.

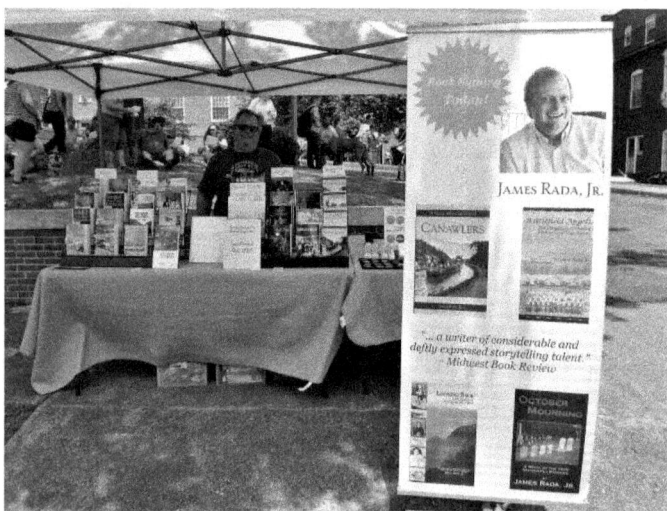

The author at a craft show with his booth set up.

Festivals can take up a lot of time, but I find them worth it. I especially like to meet with people who come see me at certain shows year after year to get my newest books.

On the money side, you can sell books at full

price or a sale price and still make a lot of money because you aren't paying retailers, distributors, or wholesalers a cut. I know an author who was mainstream published and would do shows. He had to purchase his author copies at a 40 percent discount, so he didn't have much leeway to make a profit. He sells his books at full price. Since I am indie published, I can sell my books at a sale price and still make as much profit per book as he does while selling more books because I am offering a sale price.

Networking at Writers' Conferences

No matter what type of writing you do, you can find a writers' conference that will help you learn more about your craft. While the price tag on some of the conferences may seem daunting, keep in mind that the impact of a writers' conference can continue far beyond the few days conference lasts.

Many writers attend conferences wanting to pitch their book ideas to editors and agents to get contracts with mainstream publishers or small presses. While that approach can work, you'll see more success if you first sell yourself. If editors and agents like you, they will be more inclined to work with you. You should be looking to establish long-term relationships with editors and agents who will help you produce wonderful books year after year.

While a writers' conference will bring writers,

agents and editors together, it is up to you to get the face time with an editor or agent.

Do some research before the conference to find out who is scheduled to attend and what genres they work with. Make a list of the people you want to meet in order of importance along with the person's thumbnail picture that can find on the conference material or website. You now have a cheat sheet to know whom to look for and why they would be interested in your book.

Sign up for a pitch session if it is available. These are quick pitches to a specific agents or editors. If they like your idea, they will ask for you to send more. Be friendly and excited about your idea, but don't be pushy. Again, you want to sell them on the idea that you are someone with whom they will enjoy working.

Make sure you get the person's business card. It will have all the direct contact information on it along with the proper spelling of the person's name. Once the pitch session is over, I will write any notes about the meeting and the person on the back of the card while the details are fresh in my mind. I refer to these notes when I am writing my cover letter for the package that I will send to the editor or agent.

You can also meet editors and agents informally at the various events at the conference. I know one writer who likes to volunteer as an escort at conferences. He takes the conference speakers, usually editors and agents, from room to room so they can get to their sessions on time. His escorting time also allows him a little time to pitch his book to the person.

Coming across as likable is more important for these informal meetings. People don't want to stand around talking to someone who is annoying or inappropriate. Another writer I know has pitched his book upon seeing an agent or editor in a bathroom. He hasn't been successful so far.

While editors and agents are your primary targets at a writer's conference, don't neglect networking with other attendees. Friendships developed can increase your pool of potential beta readers for your manuscript, potential reviewers, and even other authors who could provide you with a cover blurb for a future book.

Don't expect something without giving something. Be generous with your information or areas of expertise. Share information with them about markets, other writers, cover designers, etc.

Pass out your own business cards, postcards, and other promotional materials. If the conference has gift bags for speakers or for auctions, see if you can include something.

After the conference, send thank-you notes to editors and agents for their time. It doesn't hurt to follow up on any other friendships you started either.

If you are an introvert like me, it can be hard to step outside your comfort zone to network at a conference. You won't be the only person who feels that way. Just remember that everyone there is looking to make connections that can help them. Who's to say it won't be you?

Final Thoughts

You may think I've dumped a lot of information on you. I have. I've tried to give you enough information to make an informed decision about whether you want to be a freelance writer. If you do start working toward making a living as a writer, you will learn your own techniques. Additionally, forthcoming books in the Write Now! Series will explore other aspects of writing and go into greater detail.

Freelance writing is a wonderful profession, and I'm glad that I've been able to work at it for so many years. I continue to learn and get better at it. You will, too. Don't expect it to be smooth sailing to success. There will be waves that break over you and leave you feeling like your drowning. My hope is that this book will help make the waves you run into smaller.

Know that you're not alone in feeling like that. We all do at some times, no matter how long you've been in the profession.

Take the advice and tips I've provided here and try them out. Then start changing them to match your situation, your personality, your budget, etc. No one plan will work for everyone. That's why there are so many books about being a freelance writer out there.

If writing is what you want to do, then do it. Get writing, but ease into it. That way, the new lifestyle will be less of a shock to your system.

Just taking those baby steps forward will set you apart from other people who say they want to be a writer, but they don't take the actions to make it happen.

As you start to move forward in making your dream come true, you will not only run into rejection from editors, you may encounter jealousy from other "writers." I put that in quotes because, undoubtedly, those writers will be those who say they want to be a writer but don't do anything about it. They may try to dissuade you from writing or even leave bad reviews for your book.

Use that thick skin you are developing to deal with editorial rejection and use it to protect your dreams from the naysayers.

Treat them with kindness. My grandfather wasn't keen on me pursuing a writing career when I went to college. He was a businessman, and he didn't see writing as a way to make a good living. He encouraged me to pursue a business degree, and I did because I respected his opinion. I wasn't happy, though. I didn't like most of the business classes I took.

I reached the point where I knew I had to switch majors. My grandfather wasn't thrilled, but at least I had plenty of examples I could use from experience for why it wasn't for me, and when my first novel was published, he was very excited for me.

Keep your eyes and efforts on your goal and don't be dissuaded. Work at it. Work to get better, and write.

Appendix A:

Content Mills

Content mills are a good way to get started in freelance writing, particularly if you don't have experience. Consider these places as recommendations to get you started, but they are far from the only content mills out there. Once you start looking at a few of these sites, you will probably start coming across others. Look them over. You may find one that perfectly matches your interests and abilities.

Speaking of ability, as yours improves, you will probably want to move on to more selective and higher paying content mills.

ClearVoice
www.clearvoice.com

With ClearVoice, you create a portfolio on the site that clients can view and, hopefully, select you to write for them. You can also make pitches to specific clients. However, this is considered a high-end content mill, so it is more selective about who is allowed on the site, but because of this, it also tends to pay more than typical content mills.

Compose.ly
www.compose.ly

With Compose.ly, you fill out a profile that includes your experience and areas of expertise. Compose.ly will then send you projects that match your expertise and qualifications. You claim the projects you want to do and work directly with the client.

You can expect to earn between 10 and 14 cents a word for your articles, based on experience. However, be aware, the site is highly competitive, and most writers who apply are rejected.

Constant Content
www.constant-content.com

You can either offer an article you have written for sale or write one that a client of Constant Content needs.

You can set the purchase price for your own articles, but Constant Content will take a 35 percent commission. Most articles are priced around 10 cents a word with a minimum price of $7.

The advantage to you is that unlike a lot of content mills, you can write articles you are passionate about. So, if you have a particular topic you want to write about or a specialty area, this is a place where you can start to develop some contacts.

ContentGather
www.contentgather.com

This is another site where you can write the articles you want and then offer them for sale as well as writing an article on a posted topic. Unlike many sites, though, ContentGather pays in advance for articles you post. You can earn between 2 and 12 cents a word. The higher rates are for experienced writers who get high approval rates from client. At the highest level, you will automatically earn at least 10 cents a word.

Contently
www.contently.com

Contently is another site where you create an online portfolio. Clients who then need writing services can review the portfolios and find someone they want to work with.

The pay is high end, particularly for a content mill, and you can negotiate rates with the client. If you feel uncertain about doing this, you can review what similar jobs and clients have paid on Contently and ask for those amounts in your negotiation.

Crowd Content
www.crowdcontent.com

Crowd Content offers a variety of writing options including copywriting, blogs, articles, white papers, and more.

Writers can get work through the Freelance Writing Marketplace and the Managed Content platform. Marketplace writers work directly with Crowd Content clients. Managed Content writers work with in-house editors and project managers.

The pay is tiered and based on a writer's rating, but at best, you will earn 7.6 cents a word. Plan on less, though.

eByline
www.ebyline.com

eByline can list well-known clients. This is a plus if you want to list clients you have written for to help you get future work from other clients. You can also do both articles and copywriting on this site.

It can be a difficult site to get approved to work on, but it is worth it. Besides clients seeking you out through your profile, you can also make pitches to clients. You can also post pre-written articles for sale.

Scripted

www.scripted.com

Scripted is a more competitive platform, so this might be a place to wait until you have a bit of experience to apply to. They hire only 2 percent of applicants.

Once accepted, you can set your own rates. The average is around 10 cents a word.

With Scripted, clients post their project needs, which can be either an article or copywriting. You submit a proposal to them. Then it is up to the client.

There is an application fee, but it is not an unreasonable amount.

WriterAccess

www.writeraccess.com

At WriterAccess, you will probably start in the Basic Marketplace, earning 3 to 8 cents a word. As your quality improves, so will your pay. Once the company realizes you produce consistent quality work, you can enter the Pro Marketplace and earn 11 cents to $2 per word. Again, the more experience you have, the more likely you are to reach the high ends of the pay range.

Clients can also add their favorite writers to their "Love List." The company can then send offers to writers specifically on the list.

Appendix B:

Sample Query

Letters

This is just a few of the many ways you can craft a query letter, but this is a way that I have found works best for me and the articles I pitch. I show you this example as a starting point. Use this as a pattern for your first few queries, then begin to tweak it and experiment with new styles to find what works best for you.

The pattern I follow is:

- Paragraph 1 and 2 – The hook.
- Paragraph 3 – The proposal.
- Paragraph 4 – Your qualifications to write the article.
- Paragraph 5 – The wrap up and call for action.

I won't say it works every time, but it is what works for me. However, I still try different variations from time to time, either because a different style works better for the idea I'm pitching, or I want to see if I can get better results from a different version.

Case-level lede – With this type of query you narrow the broad topic of the article to focus on a particular situation as if it were a case study.

Mr./Ms. Editor's Last Name,

Mary Jenkins and John Boynton were wed in a hotel in New York in 1865. Following the ceremony, they walked out of the hotel to a large enclosure where a hot-air balloon awaited them. According to the newspaper, 2,000 to 3,000 people had paid between 50 cents and $1 to be in the enclosure, and five times that number waited in the cold outside to watch what happened next.

To the cheers of the crowd, the newlyweds rose into the air where they "solemnized" their wedding.

I would like to propose an article for *Balloon Life* called "A 19th Century Wedding in the Clouds." The article will retell the story of the 1865 wedding and all the media attention it attracted.

I am a multi-award-winning journalist and author of four historical fiction novels. I have 23 awards from MDDC, Associated Press, Society of Professional Journalists, Maryland State Teachers' Association and CNHI.

I'd be delighted to prepare this article for you. You can reach me at XXX-XXX-XXXX or by e-mail at jimrada@yahoo.com. Thank you for your time.

Sincerely,
Your Name

Salient point lede – I tied this into an upcoming event, and I mentioned previous publication in the magazine to help establish my credibility.

Mr./Ms. Editor's Last Name,
During lulls in the fighting and killing, soldiers in the Civil War decorated bullets, canteens and snuff boxes with drawings and engravings. They made game pieces out of bones and used bullets.

As the 150th anniversary of the Civil War approaches, millions of words have been written about it. "The Unwritten War: A

Visual Story of the Civil War Commemorating the 150th Anniversary of the American Civil War" shows the visual side of the Civil War with trench art, paintings, photographs and other visual artifacts that show another view of the Civil War. The exhibit will be at the Washington County Museum of the Arts from August 15 until March 21, 2010.

I would like to propose an article for *Hagerstown Magazine* called "Through the Eyes of Soldiers: Visual Arts from the Civil War." The article will look at the stories behind some of the exhibits including those with a connection to Washington County like Mathew Brady photos from Antietam and the "Portrait of Captain George Luther Hager," one of the descendants of the founder of Hagerstown.

I am a multi-award-winning journalist and author of four historical-fiction novels. In my freelance writing, I've had a number of articles published in regional and national magazines, including *Hagerstown Magazine*.

I'd be delighted to prepare this article for you. You can reach me at XXX-XXX-XXXX or by e-mail at jimrada@yahoo.com. Thank you for your time.

Sincerely,
Your Name

Combination salient point and summary lede – Notice the suggested title. It uses the subhead to combine a catchy title with explanation.

Mr./Ms. Editor's Last Name,

Have you ever read a paper in a technical journal or attended a seminar to listen to a technical expert about a startling new concept or discovery? The expert might fill the pages with charts, graphs, photos, references, and resources to convince you that his or her new concept or discovery is correct. However, when you are finished reading the article or listening to the presentation, have you ever found yourself saying, "I agree with the data, but I still can't believe what the expert's saying."

What you're experiencing is a "persuasion gap." That is, while the convincing evidence for the new concept exists, the technical expert presenting the information hasn't bridged the gap between your current beliefs and the new concept to persuade you that the new concept is correct.

I would like to propose an article for

Writing Edge called "Attitude Adjustment: Putting Persuasiveness in Technical Writing." The article will look at five ways to bridge the persuasion gap and convince readers of about your subject.

I am a multi-award-winning journalist and author of four historical fiction novels. I have 23 awards from MDDC, Associated Press, Society of Professional Journalists, Maryland State Teachers' Association and CNHI.

I'd be delighted to prepare this article for you. You can reach me at XXX-XXX-XXXX or by e-mail at jimrada@yahoo.com. Thank you for your time.

Sincerely,
Your Name

APPENDIX C: USEFUL PROGRAMS FOR FREE-LANCERS

Writers can increase their productivity using a variety of programs. Following are some of the programs I use in my work and others that authors I know have recommended to me. These are not the only programs that can fulfill the particular functions listed, but they are ones that will get the job done and well.

Microsoft Office Suite
Word Processing/Office Productivity

Every writer needs a word-processing program, and the one I use is Word. It's what I've used for years, and it does everything I need it to do. I even use it to layout a most of my books.

I use Excel spreadsheets to keep track of a lot of my projects and their progress.

I use Publisher to layout ads and a couple tabletop books I have published.

I am still using the 2013 version, and it does whatever I need. If it ain't broke, don't fix it, right? Although you can purchase an online version for a monthly fee, it is worth it to pay one price and use that version until a new version offers me something new I can use.

OpenOffice
Word Processing/Office Productivity

If you don't want the expense of Microsoft Office, you can use OpenOffice for free. It has all the programs in Microsoft Office Suite minus a few bells and whistles that you will probably only miss if you are formatting a book.

Prowritingaid or Grammarly
Grammar Check

Once you've written a book or article, you need to check it over for grammar and typos. Prowritingaid and Grammarly are two of the popular grammar-check programs out there. Both work very well. The main difference that I see is that Prowritingaid allows you to focus more on what type of check you want to put your manuscript through.

HemingwayApp
Style Improvement

Much like Prowritingaid and Grammarly can improve the technical aspects of your writing, Hemingway-App can help improve your writing style. It will help you make your writing bold and clear, and it is a free website.

Copyscape
Plagiarism Check

If you have concerns that your article might sound too similar to what is already online or even if you are worried you quoted too heavily from other people's works, you might want to run your article through a plagiarism checking program like Copyscape.

Norton
Security/Cloud Storage

You will be doing a lot of work online as a free-lance writer researching and communicating. You will want to make sure your computer is protected from viruses and hackers. While nothing is foolproof nowadays, Norton runs in the background and is regularly updated to look for new viruses. It also offers cloud storage for backing up your work in case your computer crashes.

QuickBooks
Invoicing/Bookkeeping

Since you are running a business, you need to keep track of expenses and inventory. You will also need to invoice clients and keep track of those payments. QuickBooks can accomplish it all and more. It is not cheap, but it offers a lot of reports that I check regularly to keep myself on track to reach my goals.

Square and PayPal
Payments

You will need to be able to take credit card payments. When I do shows and need to take a credit card, I use Square. Currently, it offers the lowest fees for my average sale. I have also found the reports the program sends me are easy to understand.

For online sales, I use PayPal. The fees are not unreasonable. I also like that I can create links that I connect to products on my website.

APPENDIX D: FREELANCE JOB SOURCES

While Appendix A provided a list of content mills for your consideration as a source of work, plenty of other places offer freelance writers a chance to find work.

These are just a few of the many places you can find online that are looking for writers. You will undoubtedly find more as you continue freelance writing.

Websites

- **Craigslist.com** – Most people think of Craigslist as a massive online yard sale, but it is just as massive a source of freelance writing jobs. You'll find two entries for each city – "writing / editing" under the "jobs" heading and "writing" listed under the "gigs" heading. Not every city has jobs every day or even every week. Bigger metro areas tend to have more listings than smaller areas, but sometimes you'll be surprised. Note, too, that "gigs" lets you choose to search only those jobs that claim to pay. There's a lot of criticism out there about Craigslist, but it's misplaced. Just make sure to read the listings thoroughly. I tend to search the listings under larger cities near me, but browse through other cities. You may find something that matches your interests.

- **JournalismJobs.com** – This site lists primarily full-time and part-time journalism jobs, but you can search under "freelance" or "telecommuting" and find some freelance work.

- **MediaBistro.com** – MediaBistro can be hit or miss with good freelance jobs, but it is worth a look.

- **Freelancewritinggigs.com** – This site offers just what it says it does plus other information that a freelance writer should find useful.

- **Writejobs.com** – This site has a simple layout and gets right into listing the jobs.

- **Writersweekly.com** – This site has lots of news and articles for freelancers, including market listings. The site itself also pays for articles.

Writing Associations

Writing associations usually have either a job board or will list opportunities for its author members. Most genres will have at least one organization dedicated to the genre. Here are a few to check out.

- **Academy of American Poets** – poets.org
- **American Christian Fiction Writers** – acfw.com
- **American Crime Writers League** – acwl.org
- **American Society of Business Publication Editors** – asbpe.org
- **American Society of Journalists and Authors** – asja.org
- **Authors Guild** – authorsguild.org
- **Backspace** – bksp.org
- **Historical Novel Society** – historicalnovelsociety.org
- **Horror Writers Association** – horror.org
- **Romance Writers Association** – rwanational.org

Here is a link to a page that lists these and more major writers' organizations (writerswrite.com/esources/org)

State Groups

Each state will also have its own writer's association. These groups will often sponsor conferences where you can network with other authors and editors. Like genre-specific groups, they will let members know of writing opportunities. I am a member of Pennwriters (pennwriters.org), a nationwide group that started in Pennsylvania. I have also been a member of the Maryland Writers Association (marylandwriters.org) when I lived in that state.

Here is a link to writer's groups by state, so you can find one in your area: writersrelief.com/writing-groups-for-writers.

About the Author

James Rada, Jr. is an Amazon.com bestselling author of historical fiction and non-fiction history. They include the popular books *Strike the Fuse, Canawlers,* and *Battlefield Angels: The Daughters of Charity Work as Civil War Nurses*. He also writes fantasy, horror, and middle-grade novels under the name J. R. Rada.

He has been a freelance writer since 1988. James has received numerous awards from the Maryland-Delaware-DC Press Association, Associated Press, Maryland State Teachers Association, Society of Professional Journalists, and Community Newspapers Holdings, Inc. for his newspaper writing. He has also received copywriting and magazine writing awards.

If you would like to be kept up to date on new books being published by James or ask him questions, he can be reached by e-mail at *jimrada@yahoo.com.*

To see James' other books or to order copies online, go to *www.jamesrada.com.*

PLEASE LEAVE A REVIEW

If you enjoyed this book, please help other readers find it. Reviews help the author get more exposure for his books. Please take a few minutes to review this book at *Amazon.com* or *Goodreads.com*. Thank you, and if you sign up for my mailing list at *jamesrada.com*, you can get FREE ebooks.

Keep up to date on new releases,
news, and specials from J. R. Rada
by joining his mail list at
https://bit.ly/3CILHI6.
When you sign-up,
you'll get *Polderbeest* as a FREE gift.

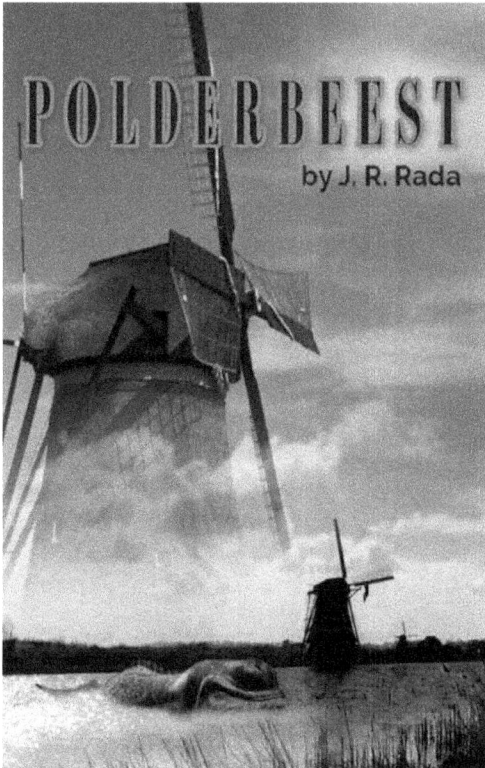

www.ingramcontent.com/pod-product-compliance
Lightning Source LLC
Chambersburg PA
CBHW070922030426
42336CB00014BA/2494